Break into Travel Writing

Beth Blair

To my husband, Jeff. May we always have adventure and laughter.

Break into Travel Writing

Beth Blair

Hodder Education

338 Euston Road, London NW1 3BH.

Hodder Education is an Hachette UK company

First published in UK 2012 by Hodder Education

First published in US 2012 by The McGraw-Hill Companies, Inc

Copyright © 2012 Beth Blair

The moral rights of the author have been asserted

Database right Hodder Education (makers)

The *Teach Yourself* name is a registered trademark of Hachette UK.

British Library Cataloguing in Publication Data: a catalogue record for this
title is available from the British Library.

Library of Congress Catalog Card Number: on file

10 9 8 7 6 5 4 3 2 1

The publisher has used its best endeavours to ensure that any website
addresses referred to in this book are correct and active at the time of going
to press. However, the publisher and the author have no responsibility for
the websites and can make no guarantee that a site will remain live or that
the content will remain relevant, decent or appropriate.

The publisher has made every effort to mark as such all words which it
believes to be trademarks. The publisher should also like to make it clear
that the presence of a word in the book, whether marked or unmarked, in
no way affects its legal status as a trademark.

Every reasonable effort has been made by the publisher to trace the
copyright holders of material in this book. Any errors or omissions should
be notified in writing to the publisher, who will endeavour to rectify the
situation for any reprints and future editions.

Hachette UK's policy is to use papers that are natural, renewable and
recyclable products and made from wood grown in sustainable forests.
The logging and manufacturing processes are expected to conform to the
environmental regulations of the country of origin.

www.hoddereducation.co.uk

Cover image © Willee Cole - Fotolia

Typeset by Cenveo Publisher Services.

Printed in Great Britain by CPI Group (UK) Ltd, Croydon, CR0 4YY.

Also available in ebook

Acknowledgements

With a grateful heart I thank everyone who contributed to *Break into Travel Writing* including...

My sources for sharing first-hand advice and wisdom: Amy Nelson, Tim Leffel, Vera Marie Badertscher, Edie Jarolim, Kara Williams, Jen Miner, Ramsey Qubein, Tim Shisler, Rolf Potts, Sheila Scarborough, Dave Sniadak, Angela England, Anna Maria Espsäter, Anya Clowers, Amanda Castleman, Benét J. Wilson, Carrie Finley-Bajak, Chris Gray Faust, Chris C. Anderson, Carolyn B. Heller, Chris Owen, Chuck Sambuchino, Charyn Pfeuffer, Deb Corbeil, Dave Bouskill, Dana Lynn Smith, Darren Cronian, Donna L. Hull, Don Ball, Don George, Candy Harrington, Catherine Bodry, Shannon Hurst Lane, Susan Farewell, Durant Imboden, Diana Rowe, Alf Alderson, Erik Deckers, G. Michael Schneider, Gary Arndt, Henry Biernacki, John DiScala, Jody Halsted, Kimberly Button, Kara Rosner, Keith Jenkins, Liz Lewis, Melissa Hart, Melanie Nelson, Mark Orwoll, Mira Temkin, Minh Tran, Maryln Hill, Nellie Huang, Paul Eisenberg, Pam Mandel, Rick Griffin, Sandi McKenna, Wade Shepard, Jen Glatt and Janet Groene. I'm honoured you took the time.

My editors at Hodder Education for their dedication and savvy editing skills and thoroughness.

My literary agent Neil Salkind for his endless enthusiasm for my writing career.

My husband, Jeff, for his support and never-ending belief in me.

My mother and father, Rex and Rita, for introducing me to reading and writing and later becoming my first editors.

My children, Jeb and Maddie. What a pleasure it is to be raising readers and travellers.

My world-travelling step-sons, Robert and William, thank you for always having curiosity and intrigue about my writing, even when you were little.

Contents

Meet the author   x

1   The life of a travel writer   1
The secret
Myths of travel writing
The allure of travel writing
Travel writer personality
A new era of travel writing
The business side of writing

2   Be the expert   21
Identify the pros and learn from them
Think back to your childhood
Look for a challenge
Find your travel expertise
Live the life
Be the authority
Climb the stairway
Image

3   Print travel writing outlets   39
Popular print: newspapers and magazines
Good readers make good writers
Books
Self-publishing
Fiction vs non-fiction
Do I need an agent?
Other writing outlets

4   Online and non-traditional opportunities   59
Websites, blogs and self-publishing
Print to online
Online travel guides
Content farms
New expectations
Mistakes corrected
Electronic books (ebooks)
Electronic applications (apps)
Digital magazines

5   Research and the press trip   75

The importance of research
What is a press trip?
Why go on a press trip?
How to make the most of your press trip
Press trip myths
Dress to impress
The unexpected costs of hosted trips
The 'no freebies allowed' rule
The joy of CVBs, tourism boards and publicists
How to interview a source

6   Pitching your idea   99

Know your audience
Anything is possible
Writers' guidelines
Query basics
An actual query
Timing is everything
Speaking of timing
After you click send...
How to connect with editors
The positive reply
Handling rejection
Other ways to get in the door
Once you get the assignment...
Plagiarism

7   Conventions and styles of writing   131

The purpose of the article
Reflective writing
Persuasive writing
Objective writing
Self-editing
Tips for proofreading your work

8   Article development   143

Outline
Title
Eye-catching beginnings
The 'meat and potatoes'
Transitions
Mastering the ending
Let's tie it all together...

9 Blogging 153

Blogs and websites – what is the difference?
What makes a successful blog?
Blogger and boss
The blogger media kit
How to make money blogging
How to write a review
Ways to promote your blog
Have a purpose
Benefits of guest blogging

10 Social media and travel writing 173

Professional benefits of social media
The balancing act
Forums

11 Photography and videos 181

The money shot
Back up
Vlogging
Professional tips

12 The importance of networking 189

Help others
Mix, mingle and meet
Have a plan
Portraying confidence
Online networking
The joy of PR people

13 The importance of self-branding 201

Who are you?
Build your bio
Branding
Planning your platform
Your personal website
What's your tag line?
Your image
Keep a media page
Recommendations
Your name
Portfolio
Business cards

14 Staying in the know and other extras   **215**

Conferences
Organizations
The future of your career
Safety first
Health
The 'green-eyed monster'
As you begin your journey...

Taking it further   **222**

Index   **225**

Meet the author

Beth Blair is a freelance travel writer, blogger and speaker. She has called 13 cities home and currently lives in the Minneapolis-St. Paul area in Minnesota, USA. Her essays and non-fiction articles have been featured in various publications and websites including *Aviation Security International*, AirTran Airways *GO*, FoxNews.com, CBSMinnesota.com, State Farm's *Good Neighbor*, *Hybrid Mom*, *Draft*, *Midwest Meetings*, *Toastmasters*, FoxNews.com, *Arizona Bride*, *Tucson Bridal*, Prime Kansas City, *HerLife*, Savvy.MN, *Arizona Daily Star*, and a dozen anthologies including *Chicken Soup for the Soul*. She was awarded first place in the 2010 Writer's Market 'Freelance Success Stories' contest and is also co-founder of the travel blog TheVacationGals.com, which won the Gold award for best travel blog in the 2012 Lowell Thomas travel journalism competition.

She has worked on and off for various airlines as a flight attendant and enjoys sharing her insider's perspective. She is frequently quoted for her travel and writing expertise in the media, including the *New York Times*, *USA Today*, *Seattle Times*, *Chicago Tribune*, *Travel + Leisure*, *Woman's Day*, MSNBC.com, FoxNews.com, AOLTravel.com, RealSimple.com and on ABC-15 Sonoran Living Live in Phoenix, Arizona and Twin Cities Live in Minnesota.

Learn more about her at BethBlair.com and connect with her in the social media world:

Twitter: @Beth Blair

Facebook: BethBlairTravels

Pinterest: TheBethBlair

The Life of a Travel Writer

In this chapter you will learn:

- ▶ *The secret to successful travel writing*
- ▶ *The myths of travel writing*
- ▶ *The benefits of travel writing*
- ▶ *What you need for your home and on-the-road offices*

When I tell people I'm a travel writer, their eyes usually light up before transforming to a dreamy, faraway look. They're most likely envisioning days spent carelessly sipping umbrella-topped rum drinks in beach chairs only steps away from fizzing white surf emerging from the turquoise horizon. Others may imagine looking up at exotic belly-dancers rolling their midsections as their bare feet move to the beat of the gentle sounding zills (finger cymbals). Or, perhaps, what comes to mind is the simple image of Tibetan prayer flags rippling in a cool breeze.

Whatever your idea of travel writing, the truth is, life as a travel writer is fun. Travel writers have done all of the above and much more. What you may not know is travel writing also takes dedication, hard work, discipline, a strong backbone, luck and a relentless desire that keeps you inspired and urges you to be the best writer you can be.

The secret

Over the years I've received many letters from strangers who have found me through my websites, articles or social media. They've all asked the same burning question: what's the secret to becoming a travel writer?

I don't want to disappoint you, but there really isn't a coveted secret. As long as you can string coherent, clear sentences you're well on your way. If you're not sure whether you have the talent or enough knowledge to write, there are numerous books dedicated to the craft of writing, some of which we will cover in this book, and there are plenty of online and in-person classes that you can invest in to help you spruce up your writing and get started in the business.

As for breaking into travel writing, each writer has their own story of how they arrived where they are today. Throughout this book you will read first-hand advice, insight and tips from professional travel writers about the craft and business of writing. You will also notice a common theme in many of the stories, including my own. If there is a secret it comes down to a combination of three things: specializing, finding the unique angle and never giving up.

Don't get me wrong, when I first began to explore the mysterious world of travel writing, I didn't realize that I was already holding the key to the magic kingdom. My original letters of introduction to editors included a generic *I'm a freelance writer...*

Sometimes, that phrase is all you need, but from personal experience, when I realized that my career background validated why I should be the one to write certain articles, my writing career blossomed. I also discovered that the more unique my idea, the better the chance I had at getting my article published. *Break into Travel Writing* is going to show how you can do the same. The goal of this book is not to offer false hopes nor to discourage you, but to provide you, aspiring travel writer, with a foundation to approach this career creatively, passionately and sensibly.

Myths of travel writing

Before we begin our *Break into Travel Writing* tour, let's address some of the misconceptions of travel writing. As with any career, it's best to avoid disappointment by understanding exactly what the profession entails before you start the journey. By the end of this book you will be able to make an informed decision on whether you would like to pursue this freelance occupation full-time, part-time or as a hobby. You will also learn why this is an exciting era for travel writers.

▶ Myth #1

Travel writers are full-time tourists. Glance at any travel writer's Facebook page and it would appear their days on the road are occupied with exhilarating moments in postcard settings. It's true that adventure is part of travel writing. That is, after all, why we signed up for this lifestyle, but such moments can be fleeting. Often, a writer's time is not their own. Instead, we're at the mercy of our host who has planned an extensive itinerary complete with lengthy interviews, resort tours and lectures on the region. All the while, we writers are furiously jotting down notes, quotes and information in between taking photos, posting on social media and collecting business cards, brochures and website addresses.

▶ Myth #2

Travel writers travel for free. As the old saying goes, nothing in life is free. Most publications do not pay for writers to travel to a destination to write about it. Staff writers may benefit from these perks from time to time, but it's rare for freelance writers to be offered an all-expenses-paid trip.

There are, however, arranged excursions for journalists on assignment or for those writers who have proven they can land an assignment. These trips are called press, media or FAM (familiarization) trips and once you've established yourself as a professional travel writer, such invitations will begin filling your inbox. Such trips have also been opening up for bloggers.

If your schedule allows for time to travel, you won't be disappointed with the trip invitations that will come your way as a travel writer. However, those invitations come with a price. That price is ensuring your work is published and seen by the world. The PR people hosting these fabulous trips anxiously await the arrival of your articles and, new to this era, watch your social media pages as you post 'live' about your experience and show photos of your experience on social media.

Warning: If you don't produce published work after the trip, your name will fall off these lists much quicker than it was added and you can kiss your press trip invitations good-bye.

As for financial burdens, incidentals at your destination, airport parking, checked luggage fees and sometimes airfare and alcohol aren't part of the press trip package.

One predicament travel writers face is that some publications have a 'no subsidized trips allowed' policy which can hinder your chance at publication if you take a press trip and wish to write about it. We'll explore this topic in more detail in Chapter 5.

▶ Myth #3

Travel writers make a lot of money. Alas, if a high income is what you're hoping to achieve, you likely won't find it in the publishing world. Before you pursue a career in travel writing, keep your day job or ensure that you have enough savings to live on. Even if you manage to work your way to landing regularly paid assignments, there is a good chance it will not be enough to live on, especially at the beginning. Competition is fierce, and freelance assignments and payment vary from month to month and from publication to publication. Plus, the increase in internet freelance work has caused the average freelance pay cheque to dwindle. Some writers have found a way to be their own boss by launching travel themed websites and blogs. We'll take a look at these options later on in Chapter 4.

It is possible to make a living as a travel writer, but you need to have a plan. The average freelance writer gets paid anywhere from $25 to $2000 (£16 to £1277) for an article and that rate is always determined by the publication. Those who get paid at the upper end of this have likely been writing professionally for many years. Freelance writers can score high commission assignments from time to time, but it's infrequent and usually not on a weekly or even a monthly basis. This statement isn't to deter you, it's simply a fact that should inspire you to work smart and find a way to make travel writing a gratifying and worthwhile job.

▶ Myth #4

Travel writers only write about travel. As previously mentioned, when you're first starting it's best to keep another steady form of income. But a secret that many travel writers have is they don't just write about travel, they cover a broad number of topics and types of writing including promotional copy, technical and other specialized and general interest topics.

▶ Myth #5

Travel writers mainly contribute to print publications. The days of print-only are long gone. Technology has officially altered the publishing world, but it's also enhanced the way travel writers work. Saving and sharing work has never been easier and email allows for instant communication. The evolution of the internet has permitted classic publications to create websites and writing entrepreneurs to launch successful privately owned travel sites and online magazines. Application software (apps) and ebooks have added a new dimension to writing opportunities, while social media provides us with easy networking as well as an outlet to the long and lonely days writers often spend behind the computer. The travel blogging trend has licensed anyone and everyone who wants their voice to be heard the chance to launch and control their own platform.

When you finish *Break into Travel Writing* you will have discovered the many outlets and avenues in which travel writers are making money. Magazines, newspapers, books, websites, blogs, ebooks, apps, social media and even photography and videos are all part of the new travel writing world.

▶ Myth #6

Travel writing is not a 'real job'. Whether travelling or writing an article, travel writers must always have their 'work' hats on. On the road, writers should be taking in the sights and sounds while searching for the perfect angle for their stories. While at home, writers must keep a tight schedule to meet deadlines and constantly be immersed in the business side of their writing career which includes marketing and selling their writing services.

The allure of travel writing

Now that we have the myths out of the way, let's discuss the positive side of travel writing. Like any job, travel writing is what you make of it. Whether you want to pursue writing as a full-time career with a regular pay cheque or whether you'd rather write just an article a month, you can direct your path whichever way you choose. That's part of the joy of working independently, although your direction will also depend upon your bills and home life situation. Regardless, if you're fresh out of school, a stay-at-home mum, an empty-nester or simply ready for a career change, you will enjoy the perks of travel writing once you are established. You may think some of the perks are frivolous or silly, but like I've said, it's what you make of it...

Travel writing offers...

- **Fun.** Travel writing is the best job in the world. Now, that is my opinion, but believe me when I say my travel experiences have brought nothing but enjoyment.

- **Flexibility.** A career as a travel writer means you have the choice of working and travelling when you wish. There aren't a lot of jobs where you can set your own hours.

- **Travel perks.** Invitations of all sorts fill my inbox, ranging from fancy events to exotic press trips. But writers also have opportunities to receive discounts on hotels, restaurants and attractions.

- **Swag.** My kids love this perk. Conferences, press trips, holidays and even 'just because' bring interesting promotional gifts from around the world. In fact, it's often a joke that travel writers never need to purchase note pads, pens and magnets because all we have to do is attend an event. (But don't ever let a gift smother your honest writing.)

- **Excitement.** No matter where you travel, you're sure to encounter some amazing experiences. From sailing to mountain climbing and everything in between, travel writing will offer you endless opportunities.

- **Reward.** Seeing your name, work and photos in print brings nothing but proud satisfaction.

- **Pay cheques.** At some point you will receive a cheque for your work. That moment will make all of your hard work worth it.

- **People.** From the moment you step into the travel-writing realm you will meet fascinating people everywhere you go. Relish these relationships.

Travel writer personality

Everyone has personality, but there's something about the freelance travel-writing career that draws the intrepid, wanderlust-filled, creative types. Our breed has the constant urge to explore, ask questions, and, as you will experience, bond quickly with other travellers and writers.

That's not to say that all travel writers are alike, but we do have some common personality traits. We have to. The reason is we're not expected to sit in an office for 40 hours a week being monitored by a boss. Travel writers must be innovative as well as clever when it comes to landing assignments because, as previously mentioned, our pay cheques are never guaranteed. During our time on the road we must be prepared for unexpected events, be flexible when plans change last minute and see challenges as the foundation for an entertaining story.

Expect your fellow travel writing comrades to be:

▶ **Curious:** Travel writers are inquisitive and always asking to learn and see more.

▶ **Active:** If you plan on travelling, being in good shape is imperative. Travel writers can easily walk miles during a research trip and it's likely you'll also have the opportunity to partake in lively activities such as cycling, skiing, snorkeling, hiking and zip-lining.

▶ **Adventurous:** You must always be ready to say yes to the next great adventure, whether it's trying a new food or learning a cultural dance.

▶ **Adaptable:** Handling any situation gracefully and tactfully is essential while travelling and writing.

▶ **Organized:** Not only do travel writers need to stay organized on the road (you may be changing hotels every night) but you also need to have a system for your workload.

▶ **Timely:** If you can't meet deadlines, this is not the job for you. The publishing industry does not have room for tardiness.

▶ **Accountable:** Whether travelling or turning in assignments, it's necessary to be reliable, on time and take responsibility for your work.

▶ **Self-motivated:** Travel writers must be able to rev their own motor because no one else is there to do it for you.

- **Business minded:** Whether you like it or not, travel writing is a business. Writers must seek paying assignments, market themselves, invoice clients and pay taxes.

- **Courteous:** Travel writers are respectful of all cultures and always aim to maintain a professional demeanor.

A new era of travel writing

Writing tools have come a long way from the sharpened-stone tools and quill feathers our ancestors relied on. Even typewriters are considered tools of the past. Writers today have advanced computer systems, tablets and other devices, such as the Dragon NaturallySpeaking voice recognition software that transcribes audio files into text files to assist in production of prose.

Our preceding generation's travel writing world consisted of sprawling travel sections in newspapers and colourful pages in glossy magazines. Those outlets still exist but sadly the pages and editorial staff are shrinking. The good news is travel writing has been taking on a new form over the last decade, thanks to the digital era, which means it's easier than ever to break into travel writing.

In fact, there has never been a more exciting time for travel writers. The publishing world today has a plethora of options and opportunities. You may pursue the classic print options of magazines and newspapers or enter the thrilling world of technology which has permitted the tech-savvy to create and sell their own travel applications, ebooks and online magazines.

Case study: Break in tips for travel writing

Maralyn D. Hill (www.theepicureanexplorer.com) a freelance lifestyle writer and author who writes for the luxury market, spas and culinary tourism.

Frequently, people wonder what it takes to break into the travel-writing industry. They see the trips and fun and don't consider the work, including writing, photographing, meeting deadlines, marketing and lining up paying markets.

Personally, I write about food, wine and travel, so I cover the components of any destination, but I do have some tips:

* The market has changed drastically since I ventured into it in 2002. I had written marketing, incentive programmes, advertising copy and the like for years, but food, wine and travel writing is different. You have to tell a story. Unless it is a guidebook, people do not want just the facts, but facts with passion and a story. I'm not putting guidebooks down, as they pay well.

* The market is inundated with bloggers, both good ones and bad ones. If you blog, which is an effective way to gain a following, be sure you write well, research, spell and use good grammar. It does matter and I'd recommend the *Associated Press Style Book*.

* If you don't have a blog or want one, guest blog on those belonging to others.

* If your writing is not up to speed, take a class.

* If you have to use free content sites to get your work somewhere, with high numbers to get started, do it. Consider it a marketing investment. Many have excellent guidelines and will not let shoddy work be published. Others don't and anything goes. I recommend the ones with stricter guidelines.

* Many paying sites only pay $15 to $50 (£9.60 to £32) an article. That means you have to write a lot of articles to make the trip worth your time.

* After a trip, I have 40 to 80 hours of work to do, as one article is no longer enough to make a trip worthwhile. Plus, going through photos takes a lot of time. Generally, I write a minimum of three to eight articles per trip, if not more.

* Starting locally with stories is a great starting point. It is also fine to use your vacations.

* Start scouring print and online publications. Ask if they use freelancers, if you can have a copy of their guidelines and editorial calendar, and what they pay. Also, do ask how long they retain first rights. Don't give your work away.

* Keep in mind that hosts for media trips need to have a return on investment. So if you can't provide it, you need to learn how.

* Hosts also want you to have an active social networking presence.

* After you have several URLs, clips, books, or apps with your byline, join a reputable writer's organization.

The business side of writing

Behind the façade of glamorous jet-setting there is a professional world, and that is the business side. If you want to be a travel writer, consider your endeavour a business opportunity. If you set yourself up for success early you will be pleased with your results.

There isn't an immediate need to spend a lot of money investing in your travel-writing career but there are some things you need to do to get started.

EMAIL

If there's one thing you're going to need as a travel writer, besides a passport, it's a professional email. Even if you already have a working email, consider opening a new account dedicated to your professional correspondences.

When picking an email name, avoid anything cute, silly or flashy. Your full name is best and don't hesitate to use a full stop or underscore if you have to. If you have a common name, like me, you may have to get creative. For example, I simply added 'writes' to the end of my name to make Beth Blair Writes. It sums up what I do for a living and includes my name – something that contributes to my personal brand, which you will learn more about in Chapter 13.

Try it now

Go online and open a new email account that is designated your professional travel writing email. Fill in the automatic signature with your name, title (travel writer), website, and contact information.

THE HOME OFFICE

With today's extensive technology options, travel writers can write wherever they are, whether it's on a train in Alaska or in a café in Beirut. But it's still nice to have a location to return to which contains all of the tools you need. While a computer (preferably with wi-fi capabilities) is the only mandatory piece of equipment you need for writing, there are a few other items that can make like easier as you begin building your clientele.

▶ A room of your own

Every writer needs to claim a space of their own. While it's not possible for everyone to have their own office with a door, having some sort of dedicated work space is imperative. The kitchen table may seem convenient, but the downside is your work will seem to take over your home which can wreak havoc on the family's harmony or annoy your roommates. Worse still, it will risk your work or computer getting destroyed by food or drink.

There are plenty of office stores that have inexpensive office furniture that is created specifically for small spaces. IKEA is an ideal place to find affordable furniture or get ideas for organizing small space.

▶ Collaborative space

For those of you who feel exasperated at the idea of setting up an office within the boundaries of your home – perhaps you have roommates who party 24 hours, a new baby, loud neighbours or find that home itself a distraction (dishes in the sink, TV to turn on, lawn to mow). If this describes you, consider signing up for a collaborative space option. You can also find collaborative space locations during your time on the road.

Case study: Co-working

Don Ball of CoCo Coworking and Collaborative Space in the Twin Cities of Minnesota offers writers some suggestions for collaborative space shopping.

> *Co-working is a movement that is bringing independent professionals and entrepreneurs together in shared workspaces, where they can work, meet and socialize. Consider it an alternative to working at home, in a coffee shop or in a leased office. Typically, 'co-workers' pay a membership fee that gives them access to the space, as well as other amenities, such as wi-fi, coffee, meeting rooms or a printers/copiers. As an out-of-town visitor, you might expect to pay a day rate or some pro-rata membership rate.*

As a travel writer, there are several advantages to working in a co-working space, including:

* **Reliable internet:** Sure, co-working spaces offer a whole lot more, but at the least you can expect a decent internet connection. This is not always the case in some hotels and coffee shops.
* **Networking with locals:** Most of your fellow co-workers are going to be local professionals and business owners, who might make excellent sources for reliable and current information on dining and destinations.
* **Focus:** Depending on how you travel, you may need to dedicate some time to concentrating on work. If so, a co-working space is ideal. While it is a social setting, most co-workers are there to get stuff done. Likewise, you will most likely find that a co-working space allows you to be intensely productive. Just remember to bring headphones or earbuds to block out any unwanted ambient noise.
* **Safety/security:** Many co-working spaces are either in locked, secure buildings or have staff on hand who ensure the safety of members and their belongings. Some spaces even offer lockers, so you can store your laptop and other valuables when you are not working.
* **A glimpse of normal:** As a travel writer, you generally interact with hospitality professionals, cabbies, tour guides and other people trying to make their living off travel and tourism. As such, you don't always get to interact with 'normal' people in your host country. Spending time in a co-working space can give you an idea of the behaviours and concerns of people who are not trying to sell you something, but are simply going about their business.

There are an estimated 1,200 co-working spaces around the world, and more are being opened every day. So chances are you will be able to find one in most major metro areas around the world, especially in wealthier countries. Not surprisingly, cities with a strong entrepreneurial scene, such as New York, London and San Francisco, have many co-working spaces to choose from. But even cities like Cairo, Egypt and Oaxaca, Mexico, have co-working spaces.

To find out whether there is a co-working space near you, you can consult one of the growing number of co-working directory services:

* Loosecubes (www.loosecubes.com)
* Desk Wanted (www.deskwanted.com)
* LiquidSpace (https://liquidspace.com).

Try it now

Walk around your home. Is there a special place you can use as your creative space? If not go online and search for co-working space possibilities in your area.

BOOKS ON WRITING

Bookshelves are lined with 'how to write' books that go into great detail about every aspect of article development including planning, writing and titling. Such books are worth the investment. Keep your library within arm's reach of your desk. Purchase books that resonate with you. Use sticky notes to mark pages and for taking notes.

PRINT, SCAN, SEND

Writers need printers and scanners for a number of reasons, the most important being signing and returning tax forms and contracts. From time to time an editor will ask for a hard copy to be mailed by snail mail, but as the industry continues to grow eco-friendly scans are becoming more and more acceptable. Until you can purchase an all-in-one printer of your own, use your local office supply store to send scans, but keep an eye out for sales while you're there. I've never paid full-price for my printer and scanner combinations.

Also invest in a pack of manila folders. Keeping some type of filing system is necessary for organizing invoices, contracts, tax forms and copies of your clips. It is best to name your files and folders generically, then at the end of the year consolidate all writing-related documents into one file with a label marking the year.

VIRTUAL ROLODEX

You've likely heard the phrase, 'It's not what you know, it's who you know...' and in travel writing this can certainly be helpful. Every time you meet someone, add them to your networking list or connect with them on LinkedIn. You never know when they may be able to connect you with someone or perhaps you can help them.

Check in from time to time to say hello, write a recommendation or, if they're local, invite them to reconnect over coffee. Chapter 12 is dedicated to efficient networking.

ROAD OFFICE

As I write this, I'm sitting in one of the many business centres in the Minneapolis-St. Paul International Airport. This space is designated to passengers in need of workspace. There are outlets for my computer charger and my mobile phone and it's rather private and quiet considering I'm in a major airport.

If you're one of those lucky travel writers who surrendered their home to experience RTW (round the world) travel, your 'office' will look a little different than those of us who have a home base. Many customer-focused retailers such as restaurants and coffee shops offer free wireless internet (wi-fi), and don't forget the co-working space option, but the more isolated your travels the less common these become. I've found that wi-fi cards or a hot-spot account such as Boingo (http://www.boingo.com/) are a godsend when I need to correspond with professional contacts. What's even better is Boingo customers can now access Gogo Inflight Internet via their Boingo account so you can fly and write on your next adventure.

Remember this

Although it is tempting to reply to professional contacts on your phone or personal digital assistant (PDA), your text can appear unprofessional as typos and grammar mistakes are likely. Try your best to respond from a computer where you can read and edit your message. If this isn't an option, some writers add a postscript along the lines of: 'Please excuse any typos or mistakes in the message, I'm currently travelling and my phone is my only email communication tool.'

PO BOX

As travel writers there are some things that need to remain private and one such thing is our home address. The best option, that I can't recommend enough, is renting a post office box. You can list this address in your email signature and on your business cards without telling the world where you nest. It also helps you keep your work and home life and mail separate.

YOUR ONLINE LIBRARY

Reference books used to be a mandatory writer need, but with the internet it's just as easy to punch in your question or verify the correct grammar. However, I still like the option of 'real' books. If you're equipped with a home office, keep such reference books on a nearby bookshelf, but on your computer add a 'writer bookmark' with shortcut links to your online collection of reference sites including www.merriam-webster.com, www. dictionary.reference.com and www.thesaurus.com. While we're talking about references, Grammar Girl (www.grammar. quickanddirtytips.com) is a wonderful resource for helping you to figure out tricky grammar rules.

Remember this

In 2009, http://MatadorU.com posted a blog post that practically went viral in the writing world. It's called 'Ten words and phrases we never want to see in travel writing again'. Among the words were *best-kept secret*, *Et cetera* (*etc.*), *gem/jewel*, *oasis/paradise* and *boast*. Such trite words will wreak havoc on your precious article and it's likely your editor will ask you remove or replace such terms. Keep your thesaurus handy as you begin your writing venture. You never know when you'll need a little assistance finding that perfect word.

Case study: Oh, the places you will go!

Travel writer Mira Temkin of Chicago (http://MiraTemkinTravel.com) describes the joys of travel writing:

> With no apologies to Dr. Seuss, being a freelance travel writer has been a fabulous way to combine my passions for both writing and travelling. It has afforded me an opportunity to travel around the world, see places off the beaten path and enjoy unique experiences I could never have done on my own.

> It gets even better when I get back to my office and start to write. How can I best share these experiences with my readers? How can I make this destination sound so appealing, people want to start packing immediately?

> The joys of travel writing can best be broken down into two categories: the wonderful experiences that become etched in your memories forever and your fellow travelling companions with whom you share the journey.

> People often ask me 'what's your favorite place?' It's hard to say because every destination brings interesting experiences. From dog

sledding and climbing down the Eiffel Tower to throwing out the first pitch at a baseball game, white water rafting, tubing, and hydroplaning, it's all good.

On a group tour, your fellow writers often add wit and wisdom as well as networking opportunities that lead to new connections and possibly even new writing assignments.

One of the challenges of travel writing is to figure out what's best to include in your article. You'll be bombarded with tons of information and photos from the Convention and Visitor's Bureau hosts ... and with print real estate being limited, you have to be objective. What best represents the destination and what will keep your reader's interest will be two of your greatest challenges. Often times, you can expand the same article online on your own travel blog.

Remember, every great journey is really about how the destination makes you feel — its history, its beauty, its art, its culture — and that's exactly what you have to share, in words and pictures, with your readers!

A BACK-UP PLAN

Many writers have stories of their computer crashing, only to realize they didn't back up their documents. Sadly, they end up having to start over from scratch. This is painful and unnecessary. Make backing up your work a habit and plan out your strategy. I use a computer back-up system that backs up my entire computer every day a certain time. I also use the online Dropbox program. It's a free service that lets you save your photos, documents, and videos from anywhere and share with others, even if my computer gets lost or stolen or falls into a swimming pool, my work is saved and can be accessed from anywhere. You may also opt to pay a little more for additional storage space. The only downfall is you must have internet access to be able to save your work – that's where Boingo or an internet card comes in handy.

PACKING CHECKLIST

Travel writers are best off using the Boy Scout mantra *be prepared*. The more you travel the better you'll get at knowing exactly what you do and don't need on your trips. Keeping a travel list on your computer will help keep you organized. Here are five categories to get you started as you organize for your next trip:

- **Must-haves:** This category represents the most important things you will need for your travels: passport, second form of ID, cash, credit cards and travellers' cheques.

- **Travel Documents:** Boarding pass, airlines, hotel and rental car confirmation numbers, contact names and numbers.

- **Electronics:** Mobile phone, computer, USB drives, outlet converter, multiple outlet plugs and camera. If you're travelling abroad, don't forget your adapter and voltage converter.

- **Clothes:** Before you pack one item of clothing, do your research. If a region is known for extreme weather or temperatures, that doesn't necessarily mean you will be visiting during that infamous time. If you're being hosted, most press trips are planned during a pleasant time of year since public relations know better than to haul a group of travel writers around in sweltering heat or the coldest months, unless the destination has a specific draw during those times. For example, trips featuring winter festivals, such as Carnaval de Québec, are only held during the chilly time of year. Therefore, know the weather before you begin to fill your suitcase to ensure you bring appropriate clothing. Also pay attention to your footwear. Nearly all press trips have a lot of walking on the itinerary. Pack your most comfortable pairs of shoes for those long days and don't hesitate to ask what the activity level is for outings. Will you be taking hikes around museum grounds, touring casinos, hiking to a waterfall or will the itinerary consist of scenic rides aboard a motor coach? Take all of this into consideration when you pack for your trips.

- **Notebook, pen and camera:** Taking notes is one of the most important tasks for travel writers while touring a new destination. Moleskine notebooks are a favourite with travel writers but use whatever is comfortable for you to jot down quotes, sites, smells, sounds and details that will help jog your memory when you're home. Even if you're not a professional photographer, taking photos as you go along will help you recall important factors and descriptions since our memories aren't always correct. As you snap photos, make notes about them. I also recommend taking photos of historic markers to help later on when you need to refer to dates and facts.

Try it now

Travellers should always keep these things with them as they fly, ride, drive or sail to their destination: medication, electronics, all forms of ID and money, important documents and laptop computers (which are not allowed to be placed in checked luggage since the lithium batteries can cause a reigniting fire).

Write your personal travel writer checklist for your checked luggage and carry-on bags to always refer to as you pack for your travels.

If you show up to your destination prepared you will feel confident, be regarded as professional and will get all you need out of your trip.

Focus points

Have a realistic view point of travel writing. Expect to work hard before you see any rewards.

Prepare for success by having the necessary tools.

Set up your personal work space.

Always back up your work.

Be prepared.

Next step

Now that you have an idea of what travel writing entails, it's time to zero in on what makes you special so you have the best chance for travel writing success. Chapter 2 will assist you as you pick your travel-themed specialty.

Be the Expert

In this chapter you will learn:

- ► *How to turn your life experiences into travel expertise*
- ► *How to learn from experienced writers*
- ► *Travel themes you can specialize in*
- ► *Why being a 'media source' can help your writing career*

Being an expert means having experience in your subject. What are you an expert in? Please don't respond with 'nothing' because everyone is an expert in something. Even if you've just graduated from high school there must be something you enjoyed doing in school or as part of your extracurricular activities.

If you've never had any serious hobbies consider this: listening to music, watching films and reading books all count as interests. And you can put a travel spin on each of these topics: music concerts are held worldwide, films are set in real locations, books all take place *somewhere*. You can relate travel to pretty much any topic you can imagine. The sky is the limit when you put your creativity to use.

Identify the pros and learn from them

Look online or watch the news and you will see that these days everyone's an expert in something, or at least claims to be. If you plan to label yourself a 'travel expert' or something similar, think about whether you have a decent amount of experience or knowledge of your subject (the old axiom 'Fake it 'till you make it' will only get you so far).

Drawing on the experience you already have can boost your confidence and make writing about your subject easy for you, while also giving you credibility. Choose to be authentic by not exaggerating your experience.

Tim Shisler (www.timshisler.com), photo and video editor at Mountain News Corporation, tackles the question, 'What is a travel professional?

> *I struggle with hobbyist vs. professional because in today's travel industry the line has become blurred thanks to digital media and the accessibility to the tools that used to have a high barrier to entry. Personally, for me, a professional is someone who is making money in return for their craft, always pursing personal development and has the same ethics and standards that one would have if working for a respected organization.*

A quick search on social media will reveal a lot of self-proclaimed travel experts, but how can you identify an actual expert and how do you compare them? And being an expert in taking press trips doesn't count. That's where authentic experience comes in.

The best way for you to identify yourself and others as experts is to look at employment background, schooling and life experiences. If you need an example, spend time surfing LinkedIn to see patterns of expertise in any field.

Tim Leffel, travel writer, editor, author of four travel books, including *Travel Writing 2.0: Earning money from your travels in the new media landscape* (2010) says he sees travel writing moving in a thousand directions.

> *The big change I see is that those who can establish themselves as an expert in a specific region or type of travel will grab a bigger and bigger slice of the revenue pie and have many more opportunities. Those me-too writers trying to be just another travel blogger or generalist travel writer are going to have a tough time making even a part-time living at this, no matter how good a writer they are. Good writing will continue to matter, whether it's informational service writing done well or narrative writing that really transports the reader and makes them feel something emotional. We're drowning in travel info at this point though, so unless you have something special to say or have more knowledge about a specific area than most, it's going to be a struggle in this increasingly crowded and fragmented reading environment.*

Nurse consultant and comfort specialist Anya Clowers (RN), is the perfect example of someone who successfully tapped her medical background to launch a successful travel-based career. She runs the website JetWithKids.com and authored the book *Jet with Kids* (2006).

Some travel writers write about travel topics but they are not necessarily an expert. Every day, journalists interview and research travel topics to develop captivating articles. Writing the article doesn't make them an expert. However, after researching, writing and studying a certain subject in-depth will transform that journalist into an expert over time.

Is there a topic you have a deep comprehension of? Were you raised in a certain environment, perhaps your grandparents ran a bed and breakfast, or do you take holidays in the same place every year? Put that knowledge and experience to work.

Case study: Talk about what you know

If you don't have the answer or knowledge, ask someone who does. Paul Eisenberg (www.pauleisenberg.com) a Lowell Thomas Award-winning journalist says:

> 'Find ways to let your readers know that while you may know what you're talking about, you don't know everything. As a father of three, I surrendered my dignity years ago, so when I write about family travel, I'm almost always starting from the place of "I learned this the hard way" or "it doesn't matter how long I travel, I always make this mistake." Likewise, just by virtue of quoting a source, you're acknowledging to your readers that you don't know everything. So one time I wanted to do a blog post about family hiking. I've taken walks in the woods with my family, but I know that doesn't make me a hiking expert. So I interviewed a hardcore outdoorsy guy who hikes a lot with his family and quoted him in the post. And for good measure, I added in the lead of that post that while I know what hiking entails, there are times when I need to turn to an expert for advice.
>
> Some writers, especially if they've been hired as a travel expert, are afraid to admit to their readers that they don't have all the answers. In my case, a little sincere self-deprecation goes a long way, and by positioning myself as a work in progress – both as a travel journalist and a person – my writing ends up being more resonant and interesting than it might otherwise be.
>
> You can certainly take this path. In fact, you can turn such a subject into an article by finding and interviewing people who are experts in your desired field. In the process, you will get an inside look at your subject and have the opportunity to ask whatever burning questions you desire.'

Try it now

Look at your resumés, social media profiles and personal bio. What key words naturally stand out and how you can relate them to travel?

Think back to your childhood

If you're lucky, you may have known your passion for a long time, as did Benét J. Wilson a self-described aviation geek since she was seven years old. 'My degree is in journalism,' she says, 'and I wrote about many different topics that I had zero interest in. In 1992, I applied for a job as reporter for a now-defunct aviation trade newspaper and never looked back.' Today Wilson is a freelance aviation and travel journalist and blogger at www.aviationqueen.com. She says writing about what you know and love guarantees you will never get bored with your topic. She goes on:

> Another benefit is that your travel writing can take you around the globe and allow you to have all kinds of great experiences, like ice skating on the second level of the Eiffel Tower, shopping in the Munich Christmas markets or flying in the bombardier seat on a restored B-17.

All of which she has done.

Look for a challenge

Often an entire market is overlooked and just waiting to be tapped. Candy Harrington editor of *Emerging Horizons* has done an outstanding job of doing just that:

> 'To be honest, I found my niche out of boredom. I had been a mainstream travel writer for about 15 years, and I was just plain tired of writing what I considered fluff. I wanted something that was a bit of a challenge, and something that I could really sink my teeth into, so I picked accessible travel. Nobody was doing it back then – some 16 years ago – and although I didn't even know anyone in a wheelchair, I knew how to research. Granted most of my colleagues thought I was a few fries short of a happy meal for making the change, but in the end it paid off well for me.
>
> I founded Emerging Horizons – *a magazine on accessible travel* – and after a disastrous first book deal decided to self-publish the first edition of Barrier-Free Travels: A Nuts and Bolts Guide for Wheelers and Slow Walkers *(2011).*

Because of my platform and some very aggressive marketing, it sold very well; and as a result I was approached by a New York City publisher to do a second edition, as well as to pen other titles on the subject. Today, Emerging Horizons is still going strong. I've authored five accessible travel books, Barrier Free Travels is in its third edition, and editors come to me when they want to cover accessible travel. I think that having a niche is essential in today's market – but pick something that can sustain your interest over the long run. Boredom is a travel writer's biggest enemy, as it tends to show through in your finished product.'

Find your travel expertise

One misconception about travel writers is that they are well travelled. Don't think that you have to have a passport full of stamps to kick off your travel writing career. You can start in your own backyard or, better still, look at some spheres you call or could consider calling your own. The following list is hardly exhaustive, but it should offer a nudge of inspiration. As you read, relate each topic to your life and imagine how you can take it a step further.

▶ **Backpacking:** Backpacking across Europe is frequently called a rite of passage for young people, but as you dig into the various travel writing niches you'll discover that people of all ages are touring the world with a backpack. Backpackers can take a number of forms: the traveller who literally hits the road with a backpack, staying in hostels or campgrounds along the way or they may opt for more luxurious accommodation, stay with friends or a little of all of the above.

▶ **Expat:** Abbreviated from the word *expatriate*, expats have temporarily or permanently relocated to a new country which is often drastically different from where they were raised.

▶ **Solo:** Venturing out into the world without a companion may seem intimidating, but it forces you to have a much different experience than if you were distracted by others' needs and desires. Elizabeth Gilbert's memoir *Eat, Pray, Love* (Viking, 2006) is a perfect example of a solo traveller's experience turning into an astounding success.

▶ **Young adults:** The late teens and early twenties mean different things for different people. For some, experiences involve couch-surfing, hostel stays and the best 'happy hours', while for others the focus is college credits, quiet coffee houses and used book stores. If you are young, consider yourself fortunate because you're in an ideal position to claim a niche and run with it. And don't be surprised when your interests evolve as you age.

▶ **Boomer travel:** Boomer travel has been taking off over the last decade as the 'boomer generation' become empty-nesters, retiring and travelling the world. This group travels with their partners, friends and their multigenerational families. Websites like www.grandparents.com and www.GrandMagazine.com are perfect examples of online publications written for this active population.

Writer and blogger Donna L. Hull explains:

> *'In today's world, a new travel writer benefits most from establishing a niche, allowing him or her to stand out from the crowd. It also broadens market possibilities beyond the typical travel publications. For instance, by writing about active travel for baby boomers at http://MyItchyTravelFeet.com, I've attracted freelance writing assignments from companies that publish general content for baby boomers.'*

▶ **Family:** Family travel has always been a hot topic. Unlike other topics, family travel takes a lot of planning and budgeting. The key here is to delve into what your experiences are. Since the 'mum blogging' world has ignited, so have the number of family travel blogs. Don't be intimidated or try to compete with the other mum bloggers out there. As with any topic, you will notice the same themes and article titles on almost every blog. Tips like travelling on airplanes, road trips, child proofing hotel rooms, dealing with sick kids on the road, travelling internationally and packing for a holiday come up again and again, and most of the time it's the same information being regenerated over and over. Instead, focus on your family life. What makes you different? If you're a hockey, football or any other sport mum with children on a travelling team, you could contribute to youth sport magazines or start your own blog on the topic of travelling to sports games. You can focus on family-friendly restaurants, hotels and other attractions for other sports team families. Or you can concentrate on children's health needs by writing about travelling with children with allergies, children with autism or gifted children.

▶ **Multigenerational:** Take family travel to the next level by including extended family, mainly grandparents, on your holidays. Trips with family members of different generations take a special type of planning, since energy and activity levels vary.

▶ **Theme parks:** Visit any theme or amusement park and you will discover that some families' annual holiday consists of only theme or waterparks. It's not uncommon for families to plan the same trip year after year. If this sounds like your family, consider specializing in certain aspects of the parks, such food, entertainment, lodging or family-friendly features.

▶ **Spas:** Ooh, la, la... Who doesn't love to spend a relaxing day or week at a spa? Spas and health resorts are located around the world. Topics can range from your local gym's massages to a week-long stay at an all-inclusive health spa.

▶ **Practical travel:** This is the one aspect of travel writing that applies to nearly all travellers. General travel information, insider information, first-hand tips and advice on topics such as air travel, hotels, luggage, frequent-flyer information is easily classified as 'practical travel' writing.

▶ **Niche:** Travel journalist Ramsey Qubein has tailored his writing to certain markets:

'I focus mainly on business travel, which includes airlines, hotels, airports, and destinations. I do cover leisure travel as well especially in terms of providing meaningful content for both a travel agent and a consumer audience. Yes, there are still travel agents out there who are thriving because they specialize in a niche like safaris, cruises, etc. Pick a niche, and you can really excel. Within my travel writing, I have a special focus on the Middle East and Africa covering business and leisure travel to those markets, but I also write a lot about Europe and Asia. I love the variety!'

▶ **Culinary:** One of the most brilliant marketing plans in the United States was the launch of regional culinary trails. These are mapped 'trails' in the area focusing on regional specialties. I've partaken in several, including Arizona's Salsa Trail and Lake Charles, Louisiana's Seafood Sensation. But you don't have to stick with a trail to find delicious food stories.

▶ **Spirits:** Along the same lines as above, one of my favourite trips was experiencing the Bourbon Trail out of Lexington, Kentucky, and of course there is the quintessential wine destination Napa Valley. A quick online search will reveal that many people like to specialize in this topic. Beer connoisseurs, wine lovers and cocktail imbibers have staked their claim on these topics, but don't feel intimidated. There's always room for more. Brainstorm what about the topic interests you and run with it. Think festivals, brewery tours, tastings or any other creative beverage angles like coffee or tea that you can expand on.

▶ **Gay travel:** The gay and lesbian and other alternative lifestyle communities are a terrific travelling group and make for an ideal market for travel pieces.

▶ **Adventure:** If finding that adrenaline rush thrills you to no end, well you've likely found your subject. Sky diving to scuba diving, the choice is yours as you tap into the exciting sports and activities that get your blood pumping. The more often you participate in such adventures the more qualified an expert you become.

- ▶ **Airlines and aviation:** These topics are near and dear to my heart since my background is in the airlines. Aviation enthusiasts can easily become immersed in their topic. If flying as a subject piques your interests but you don't think you're knowledgeable enough on avionics, fear not. Take a look at the big picture. Focus on anything related to aviation. Air shows, air and space museums, inflight trends, airport store openings and newsworthy topics are examples of trending topics that are covered regularly.

- ▶ **Round-ups:** *Top Tens*, *Best of...* and *Most Popular* articles circulate year-round, changing with the seasons, from latest crazes to traditional favourites. There are writers who have made entire careers out of compiling such lists.

- ▶ **Sports:** If you're an athlete, this is the perfect way to tie in your sport and travel writing. For example, if you're a runner, focus on races, scenic places to run or the best restaurants to carb-load before the big race. The same goes for cyclists, swimmers and walkers. Or, perhaps your experience and enthusiasm revolves around snow play, such as skiing or snowboarding, or the other extreme sports, such as paddle boarding, surfing or snorkeling. Travel your sport. Before you know it, you'll be the go-to person to cover the latest buzz in your sport.

- ▶ **Homeschooling:** If you're involved in the homeschooling world, specializing in travelling for homeschoolers can cross another of topics from near and far field trip ideas to history lessons.

- ▶ **Outdoors:** Considering there is an entire magazine dedicated to this topic, there is a good chance you can find plenty to write about in this field. Skiing, camping, hiking and hunting also have magazines dedicated to their appropriate topics. If you have any experience in any of these activities, you already have a head start.

Freelance writer Alf Alderson (http://alfalderson.co.uk) turned his love of surfing into a successful writing career. Not only does he write for various print and online publications but he has also written several books on surfing. His latest tome is *Ultimate Surfing Destinations* (2010), a coffee table book. His impressive surfing specialty opened the door to the other extreme, writing about skiing. He is also the co-author of the *Rough Guide to the Rocky Mountains* (2002) and he writes a regular blog and features from the Alps – where he's based for the ski season – for http://welove2ski.com.

Alderson says, 'I like to think I've achieved this through hard work always meeting deadlines and providing copy and pictures as requested, and building up good working relationships with often busy and pressurized editors, which isn't always easy.'

▶ **Girlfriend getaways**: Like 'chick lit', the female travel market is pretty new but here to stay. Ladies love their girlfriend time and it's reflected in the upswing in popularity of these specialized trips.

▶ **Accommodation**: Everyone has to sleep, but not everyone looks for the same thing in a hotel. Families on a budget will most likely book hotels with free breakfasts, while wealthy professionals may be looking for hotels with leisure facilities. There are plenty of luxury writers out there, and who can blame them? But maybe your specialty is bed and breakfasts or cabins. Then there is the hostel world. If you've stayed at more hostels than you can count, you most likely know what to look for when comparing a city's hostels. Is breakfast included? Is there a curfew? Are the rooms private or dormitory style? Use your experience and start writing. Start with a round-up of your favourite amenities, rules or actual hostels and see what descriptions and life you can breathe into the article.

▶ **Weddings and honeymoons**: If love makes you feel all sappy inside, this may be the right topic for you. There are always publications – and even jewellers – looking for creative or romantic engagement stories. The story of my personal engagement in *Chicken Soup for the Brides' Soul* (Health Communications Inc., 2004) led to a number of published wedding clips in several print magazines.

Case study: follow your passion

Freelance writer Vera Marie Badertscher travels when she can, and reads travel literature when she isn't travelling. Her website, http://ATravelersLibrary.com, combines these two interests with literature that inspires travel. She explains how she found her corner of the internet:

'The blog was a response to feeling that I was kind of out of it concerning the Internet and needed to sharpen my skills. I started A Traveler's Library because my two main interests are literature and travel and because I noticed that whenever someone asked a question in a travel forum about "What book should I read before I go to X?", there would follow a very lengthy discussion. Obviously there was a lot of interest and I couldn't find anyone filling that little niche. So three years ago I took the plunge. I love blogging and it has gradually taken over my life. Finally, the economy has made it so difficult to place articles in print magazines that I am much happier being my own boss and writing what I like, rather than beating my head against the wall of rejection.'

Melissa Hart (http://Melissahart.com) of Eugene, Oregon, is a freelance writer and contributing editor at *The Writer Magazine*, and the author of the memoir, *Gringa: A Contradictory Girlhood* (2009).

'I've worked as a freelance travel writer for magazines and newspapers for several years. My career really took off when I found myself immersed in wildlife rehabilitation as a hobby and a passion. I began to travel to other rehabilitation centers across the country, and then across the world. I was able to report on them with insight because of my own volunteer work. My best advice to travel writers is to pursue a passion aside from travel — snowboarding, quilting, homeschooling, whatever — and then travel to places that offer a new and interesting take on this passion.'

Live the life

Rolf Potts, freelance travel writer and author of *Vagabonding: An Uncommon Guide to the Art of Long-Term World Travel* (2002) explains why writers should try to develop an expertise:

> 'I always say to read a lot, write a lot and travel a lot. And travel well. This means you'll have to do a lot of travel – deep, intensive, eyes-open travel – on your own dime before people will start paying you to do it. Often the best way to build this kind of expertise for international destinations is to move overseas to work a day job as an expat or a digital nomad.'

For some people, moving isn't an option. This means you need to be practical in the type of travel writing you wish to get involved in. For example, if you want to see the world but don't have enough cash saved up for travelling, consider the different types of career that can give you insider knowledge of a travel topic. If you're single, working for a cruise ship can present endless opportunities to see the world and give you insights into types of places and topics that interest you. In fact, any seasonal occupation can offer the same benefits. National Parks, ski resorts and beachside towns can develop you into a pro over one or two seasons.

Be the authority

If you have the courage to write authoritatively you will have no problem commanding the respect and attracting the assignments you desire and deserve. Most importantly, remember, if you don't have the answer ... find someone who does.

Even experts don't have the answer to everything. As time moves on, facts, figures and statistics change; that's why it's important to stay up to date with the latest news and information in your niche's industry. Read the newspaper, or news sites, trade magazines and attend relevant conferences. The more you stay current with cutting edge information the more in demand you will be.

Case study: Claiming your niche

Ten years ago Chris Owen fell in love with cruising and started a website http://LifeIsCruising.com. Eventually that passion led him to become a travel agent. Today he's one of the top travel cruise experts in the blogosphere writing for his own site www.chriscruises.net and AOL's travel site www.gadling.com.

'My stint as a travel agent taught me a great deal about the business end of travel. Already established as a source of cruise information before that, I found that adding insider information to the mix propelled me more into writing about it and offering unique content not found elsewhere.

I have four key tips and areas of concentration for self branding and these things have served me well in a number of careers: Study. Experience. Become consumed. Have patience.

To be an expert at anything one must know a great deal about it, but not necessarily have to know everything. I think that's one of the biggest mistakes people make for a couple of reasons. First, nobody likes a "know-it-all" and a would-be expert needs people to like them. Being liked will open doors for opportunities.

Let somebody else be the one who can quote numbers if you are not good with numbers. For example, cruise industry expert Stewart Chiron (cruiseguy.com) knows all the cruise ship numbers: how many people they hold, when they were built, etc. He is never wrong and carries that information around in his head. I can't do that and focus on the experience of cruising and what others might need or want to know about it.

Personal experience is key. That's what blogging is about and the more experiences one has to share, the more interesting they are to readers. At the end of the day there has to be a reason for doing it other than seeing your byline published someplace. When I finish writing something, anything, I read it and ask myself, "Why did I write that?"

Along with the personal experience comes the being consumed thing. It's a thing a blogger has to do or they are doomed. Travel consumer advocate Chris Elliott said at a seminar I attended that to be successful you have to write every day. He said if you can't write a post every day on your topic, you're writing about the wrong topic. I agree with that.'

Climb the stairway

Starting with a specialized theme will allow you to make your way up the publishing chain no matter where you start. As long as you begin somewhere: blogs, websites, local publications, regional publications, national publications, books ... you can go as far up as you desire.

KEEP A MEDIA PAGE

If you've appeared in the media, sharing your expertise, then let the world know on your website's media page and link to the proof. Once you're validated as an expert in a subject, landing assignments will get easier and easier.

If you're new to this world, this is how it works. There are several online services that allow journalists to post a call-out for sources to contribute to their latest story. The emails are filled with a long list of requests from various journalists and writers and are sent out via email weekly, or as much as one to three times a day, to people who have signed up. Sources who feel they can assist the journalist will reply directly to the writer with their thoughts, comments and advice. If the journalist feels the person is a good match they will contact the source and move forward with their story. The situation is a win-win for everyone.

This is an uncomplicated way for you to brand yourself as an expert, and possibly get a mention for your own website or blog, and it is a fabulous tool for writers to use when searching for that perfect source to enhance an article.

There are many options out there to choose from including:

► www.helpareporter.com (Help A Reporter Out (HARO))

► http://ReporterConnection.com

► http://TheSourceBottle.com

► http://TravMedia.com

Go to Chapter 13 for more information on maintaining a media page.

Try it now

Sign up for any or all of the sites listed above to look for opportunities to boost your expert status.

TIPS FOR BEING A GOOD SOURCE

▸ **Be available:** Responding to emails and answering the phone may seem like obvious ways to be available, but you'd be surprised how many times I have had people offer to contribute to a story only to be absent or unresponsive when the time comes.

▸ **Be helpful:** After you supply your thoughts, offer to expand if needed or assist with any future articles.

▸ **Write or talk in sound bites:** Sound bites are brief statements that quickly get to the point. The news media uses this tactic to grab viewers' attention when time is limited. Do the same for a verbal or email interview. An interview sound bite is like a neatly wrapped gift for journalists. All the interviewer has to do is open the package and place it into their story's text. The better source you are, the more likely the media will continue to ask for your input. If you end up writing articles that cite sources, you will see how appreciated well thought out quotes can be.

▸ **Offer unique information:** Some topics bring the same response time and time again, but if you're always looking for creative angles or the latest information you will become a media gem.

Image

We often hear the phrase 'show, don't tell' when writing, and this phrase is especially true in travel writing and when moulding your image. Show that you're a travel writer by including photos of your travels on your website and social media pages. If you specialize in a certain genre of travel writing, for example adventure travel, post photos of your exciting feats, whether it's climbing Kilimanjaro or taking part in a local canoeing contest.

Focus points

Choose a subject you're passionate about.

Put effort into becoming an expert on the subject.

Let the world know you're well-versed in the topic.

Show the world what you have to offer.

Take the first step and before you know it you'll have miles of pages behind you.

Next step

As an expert in your subject, it's time to put your subject knowledge to use. Despite rumours that print is dead, such assignments are still available. Chapter 3 will explain how you can land assignments in newspapers and magazines and get access to the assigning editors.

Print Travel Writing Outlets

In this chapter you will learn:

- ▶ *What print assignments are out there*
- ▶ *What editors are looking for*
- ▶ *The value of offering photography*
- ▶ *What to look for in your contract*
- ▶ *What it takes to write a book today*
- ▶ *The pros and cons of self-publishing*
- ▶ *Whether you're ready for a literary agent*

If there's one thing you take away from this book, in writing for print or online, remember to write about what you love. Otherwise, your writing will suffer and the excitement you had when you first started will diminish. Writing will feel like a chore rather than a fun occupation. And that is why it's important to indulge yourself with topics you are interested in, or better yet, passionate about.

Fortunately, not all travel writing is created equal and not all writers have the same gifts. In other words, travel writing spans a variety of topics from personal experiences to destinations geared towards a specific crowd to practical travel written by industry insiders. Once you recognize where your interests and talents lie you will have no problem having your work accepted by print publications. But first you must hone your craft, build your strengths and identify your talents.

Try it now

Sometimes we get stuck in a job that is soul-sucking and we lose our zeal for life. Now is the opportunity to recapture what excites you.

Look around your home or office...
* What print publications do you read?
* What are your hobbies?
* What topics can you discuss extensively?
* What websites do you read?
* What sports do you play?

The answer to each of these questions will reveal something about you and give you hints on what direction you should take.

Now, write about something travel related that you love. Think back to your childhood and recall your dreams, favourite holidays, summer experiences and school field trips. Reconnecting with the feelings that accompanied these events will help you recapture your enthusiasm for your favourite subjects. Write something, anything. Describe a place or tell a story. Do this every day.

Popular print: newspapers and magazines

Some writers debate whether there is any point writing for print magazines today since the internet has made publishing so easily accessible. If your plan is to work full-time as a freelance travel writer, receiving regular pay cheques, then you will absolutely want to write for print publications.

Mark Orwoll, International Editor of *Travel + Leisure* describes the changing face of travel journalism:

> 'In today's travel journalism – in fact, in journalism of all stripes – there is an increasing emphasis on immediacy over consideration, on service information over experience, on brevity over depth. That's not a complaint, just an observation. But there are benefits to these changes. Readers expect and receive much more timely travel news through blogs and social media. They expect and receive advice about prices, rip-offs and insider secrets in a much more concrete way. They expect and receive information written in a way that allows them to get as much detail in as small a space as possible so that they can continue absorbing the constantly increasing mass media that more or less assault them daily. There are still places for thoughtful, experiential, long-form travel journalism, though, so we don't have to hold a literary funeral service just yet.'

Mark Orwoll continues:

> 'Print is still the Holy Grail for most writers. It's where the prestige (and bigger pay cheques) can be found. So yes, writers should try to break into print—if they have the reporting and writing skills that qualify. To make a very broad statement, the best quality travel journalism is found in print, and the very best writers end up there. A writer whose calibre of work is high enough will eventually wind up in print – and everywhere else.'

Despite the elimination and reduction of some travel sections, the 'eye-candy' sections still do exist and while it may take some time and coaxing, you can still get your name in them. Similar to other print publications, study the newspaper and have a strategy. There is a good chance that while the newspaper may be mostly staff written, the online contributions may be open to anyone.

Magazines have always been an attractive place for writers to submit work and print magazines are where the best pay cheques come from. These mostly pay by the word or a flat fee for shorter pieces. Magazines are everywhere we look. When it comes to writing for magazines, strategy is also helpful and one of the best is starting at the bottom and working your way up the ladder. Local publications are the easiest to break into, and then regional and so forth. It is then easier to work your way into the larger circulation and higher paying publications. I can say from first-hand experience that there is no better feeling as a writer than to hold a glossy magazine that features your story.

Traditional print newspapers are still the typical daily or Sunday newspapers we grew up with, even if they're a little thinner than we remember. Newspapers normally pay a flat fee per piece depending upon length.

Freelance writer Jen Glatt (jenglatt.com) offers novice writers her top three tips:

1 Be open to the fact that opportunities are everywhere to travel write. Your backyard may be on someone's travel bucket list, and who better to write about a place than a local?

2 Never pass up an opportunity to have a conversation with someone you don't know.

3 A travel writer travels, regardless of whether she's being paid to travel. Curiosity about the world is essential.

LOOK LOCAL

Starting with regional publications is some of the oldest advice in the travel writing, but it's good advice for a reason. You know your surroundings, weather, wildlife and culture better than any outsider. You have two choices: to offer your work to a local publication or to pitch your knowledge of your area to other publications.

If you're currently still in education, you may have an automatic 'in' with your college or university's local publication. Otherwise, there is likely to be at least one community publication in your area. Study the publication and see what is missing. Perhaps the periodical could benefit from a section on day trips, spring break tips or local summer events?

Don't pigeonhole yourself into only approaching travel markets. Every city and town has a list of publications that travel can fit into. Look for local publications everywhere you go: the supermarket, doctors' surgeries, schools, libraries, restaurants and airports. Topics may be:

▶ Parenting

▶ Sports

▶ Health and Fitness

▶ Community

▶ Outdoors

▶ Self-improvement

These are some types of publication that are likely to be accessible to you:

Local magazines: These focus on your immediate region, and will probably have your city or town's name on the cover and focus on community or city stories. *Minnesota Monthly* and *Savvy.MN* (Minnesota) are two of my local publications.

Regional magazines: These are marketed in a larger area, and include titles such as *Midwest Living Magazine in the US*, and the *Dalesman in the UK*.

National magazines: These include titles such as *National Geographic Traveller* and *Condé Nast Traveller* (both published in the UK and the US).

START LOCALLY, GROW GLOBALLY
Since financial assistance isn't likely when you're first starting out, new travel writers should approach their travel writing creatively. When you're first launching your travel writing career it's likely

you won't have the funds to jet off to several exotic locale at will; that's why starting local can help boost you into the travel writing world. This isn't a new tactic. In fact, some writers have become so successful in regional writing they only specialize in their local area.

An inflight publication I wrote for preferred local writers to cover their travel pieces because they knew they were getting an insider's perspective rather than someone who only saw the surface for a few days. Don't take this advice lightly. You will be pleasantly surprised at how many assignments come your way as a beginner if you can focus on your local area. You will then have a nice display of clips to show editors and PR people when the time comes to start travelling.

TRADE MAGAZINES

Magazines written for a designated industry are called trade magazines, and they are one of the best-kept secrets in the freelance writing world. Not only do these publications pay well but writing for them can enhance your credibility.

Whether your background is restaurants, medicine or cars you can find magazines to write for in your field. You will also find travel-themed publications such as *Student Group Tour Magazine, Business Travel News, Smart Meetings, Motorcycle Classics, Boutique Design* (boutique hotel, spa and restaurant market) as well as a number of others covering aviation, and travel-themed conventions and trade shows.

Be available: a couple of years ago I answered an urgent call-out in a travel writers' newsletter for a meetings trade publication whose writer had backed out of an assignment at the last minute, and whose editor needed a feature story within a week. Because I was from the region I won the assignment and walked away with a nice cheque.

Good readers make good writers

Spend a few minutes reading every day. Since your interest is obviously travel, pick up a classic like *The Great Railway Bazaar* (1975) by Paul Theroux as well as a modern book such as *Into the Wild* (1997) by Jon Krakauer which tells the story of a young man by the name of Chris McCandless who abandoned his identity to travel and explore Alaska.

In addition to the endless travel books available, read magazines, newspapers and websites. Observe the different styles and types of travel writing. You will notice that travel writing isn't limited to feature articles about the latest tropical paradise or newest cruise ship.

As you browse the shelves in bookshops or libraries, take note how travel writing has a long history as a genre. Age-old writers blazed the path for us modern writers, with their unique perspectives of the eras they were living in. Lady Mary Wortley Montagu (1689–1762), wife to the British ambassador to Turkey, is considered one of the world's first women travel writers. She's known for her letters from Turkey which relay her journeys through Europe in 1716. Her recollections were later published as *The Turkish Embassy Letters* (1763).

Heinrich Harrer (1912–2006) is best known for his autobiographical travel and adventure books: *Seven Years in Tibet* (1952), which depicts this time he spend in Tibet getting to know the fourteenth Dalai Lama, and *The White Spider* (1959) which covers his experience as one of four climbers who first scaled the North Face of the Eiger in Switzerland. Harrer's adventurous spirit and ability to retell his personal encounters leaves writers inspired and in awe.

> 'Wherever I live, I shall feel homesick for Tibet. I often think I can still hear the cries of wild geese and cranes and the beating of their wings as they fly over Lhasa in the clear cold moonlight. My heartfelt wish is that my story may create some understanding for a people whose will to live in peace and freedom has won so little sympathy from an indifferent world.'

Seven Years in Tibet *by Heinrich Harrer*

As already pointed out, not all travel writing stays within the limits of pondering memoirs; it can be knee-jerkingly hilarious as Bill Bryson has proven. His first travel book *The Lost Continent: Travels in Small Town America* (1990) chronicles his experiences during an American road trip. In his next book, *Neither Here Nor There* (1993) he recounted his first tour of Europe.

Memoirs, essays, practical travel advice, destination guides, travel news, themed pieces and events are all different classifications of travel writing. By recognizing the different forms you will also begin to recognize the style you prefer to write.

Try it now

Let's clarify something. Not everyone is good at every type of writing. Some writers naturally produce descriptive prose, while others are gifted at reporting the latest travel news. Your next task is to dabble in different styles of writing, in the hope of discovering what style you write best.

Perhaps you're brilliant at bringing a destination to life on paper through personal expression, or maybe your talent is uncovering historic facts. As you begin, write about what you know but also explore subjects that are new to you. You may uncover a talent or aptitude you didn't know you had.

Recall a funny moment from your childhood or adult travels. Sometimes what doesn't seem funny at the time can make wonderful fodder later. Have you ever experienced a flat tire on a road trip, encountered a wild animal, been stranded in an airport? Maybe you have discovered a tarantula on your hotel pillow or been assigned to a room which was already occupied. Every odd situation you've experienced can be brought to life on paper in an entertaining fashion.

Now turn one of your experiences into a short passage: After choosing your memory, write about the situation from a comic standpoint. It is okay to make fun of your own reaction (you screamed like a child when you saw the spider) or embellish the situation (describe the tarantula as the size of an octopus).

Next, take the same situation and recall it as if you learned something profound from the situation or write from an educational or how-to standpoint. Maybe the situation made you want to explore the region's wildlife further, or at the other extreme, perhaps it taught you to not skimp on hotel lodgings to save money. Or you can share with your reader what they should do if they do find an arachnid in their room.

Books

Being a published author is every writer's dream. And why not? The projected prestige, glamour and sky-high advances we hear about in the news make book writing sound dreamy and a guaranteed ticket to career and financial success.

While writing a book can give your career a jolt, most writers don't experience the fame and fortune that a select few amass. But writing a book can boost your credentials, lead to other published books, speaking gigs, TV appearances and a whirlwind of other career opportunities. And you get to say you're a published author.

One thing I've learned while writing this book is that any time the subject came up that I was working on this title, there was a good chance the person or people I was chatting with, professional writers or not, talked about 'their' book idea.

What most burgeoning authors don't realize is, unlike getting articles published, writing and getting a book published takes a plan. Most book authors take years to build a platform, plenty of published articles and, most importantly, a unique book angle.

Since the internet has stolen a lot of the publishing world's glory, publishers are forced to reject many good ideas that would easily have been published five or ten years ago.

Travel books run the gamut from first person stories to traditional guidebooks. Just like articles, writers are drawn to the different types of writing. The following are the most popular types of travel book on the bookshelves today.

- ▶ **Narrative**: Travel literature and travelogues normally fill the bookshelves in the travel sections. Authors relaying their personal tales of adventures, encounters and self-discovery in new lands produce fascinating reads and often inspire the reader to want to venture out on their own escapade.

- ▶ **Guidebooks**: Travel guides are written to assist the reader during their journey. Frommer's, Fodor's, Lonely Planet, Moon Handbooks and Rough Guides are all examples of print guidebooks (each publication also has an online version). Such guides specialize in a region and reveal helpful solutions, advice and itineraries for tourists. There is much speculation about the life expectancy of guidebooks due to the popularity of websites and electronic applications. Nevertheless, they are still being published and writers can still apply to write the next version of many popular guidebooks.

▶ **Specialist 'how-to':** Books dedicated to certain practical travel topics fall into this category. Unlike guidebooks, which usually list attractions, hotels and restaurants, these books unveil helpful information that can make travel less stressful. An example of this type of book is *The Wall Street Journal Guide to Power Travel: How to Arrive with Your Dignity, Sanity, and Wallet Intact* (2009) by Scott McCartney. The pages are filled with insightful advice given by a professional traveller.

Most book contracts involve an author advance and book royalties. Some guidebooks pay only a flat fee. Authors writing a narrative or specialist 'how-to' book should expect to use an agent to assist in finding a publisher for their project. Guidebook writers can usually approach the publisher directly or apply for a book assignment through the publisher's website.

Case study: Guidebook writing

Catherine Bodry (www.catherinebodry.com) is a freelance travel and adventure writer and a Lonely Planet guidebook author.

'That's my dream job! How did you get it?' I hear variations of these thoughts often when I tell people my job titles: Travel Writer. Lonely Planet Author.

At first, I answered the question kindly. I told them the truth: 'I got the job with luck and perseverance.' I knew that I wanted to work for Lonely Planet, and never really believed I actually could, but I was very lucky that Lonely Planet was specifically looking for a writer in my region.

Now, however, I sometimes find myself giving a more snarky answer: 'I applied.' This answer is not just because I hear the question over and over, but because it's often asked with such awe. But what I want to convey is that it's just a job, and I got it like you get any other job. I went to the Lonely Planet website, saw what their qualifications were and set about filling them. (I hadn't been published yet and they require three published clips. So I got published in a free bi-monthly magazine that, quite honestly, will publish anyone. I didn't get paid, but I made sure my writing was good even if the publication wasn't.) Then I applied, wrote a sample chapter like they asked, and was lucky enough to get in to the author pool.

It was really as simple as that.

Something else I try to convey to the starry-eyed travelers who think I have their dream job is that it's not always dreamy. The pay is low. You have to travel like a backpacker, even though you're a 30-something with a graduate degree. I spent three nights in my sleeping bag on the deck of a ferry this summer while doing guidebook research. I slept in my tent four nights out of five. In Asia, I lost five pounds from walking and sweating. I itched from insect bites and sun burn. I rarely went out on the town, because I had to be on top of my game the next day, walking and being perky and trying to get information from people who couldn't understand me – or I them. I am definitely, definitely not being paid to take a vacation.

Despite the realities of the theoretical dream job, however, I have to say that it's still my dream job. It just suits me so perfectly: I crave variety and stimulation and can't do office work for more than a couple of months at a time without going stir crazy. In guidebook writing, every day is different. You're constantly pushing your boundaries and limits – seeking out new places, new foods, new adventures. Your constitution is constantly tested, and you feel stronger when you realize what you're capable of. You make friends. You're forced to smile a lot, but it feels good.

Guidebook writing, like good hard travel, has made me realize that I am capable and competent, and there's no greater reward from a job. Except, of course, a giant pay check.

Self-publishing

Some of my favourite authors have histories of self-publishing. Today it's easier than ever but before you make a decision it's best to weigh the pros and cons of each.

▶ **Pros**

▶ The project is 100 per cent yours.

▶ You choose the book title.

▶ You design the cover.

▶ Self-published books can be produced quicker than traditionally published books.

- You earn all of the profits.

- No more pitching to agents or publishers.

- Self-publishing can lead you to a book deal with a traditional publishing.

- **Cons**

- You have to spend money upfront.

- You need to pay an editor.

- You're on your own for marketing.

While self-publishing a print book is always an option, Chapter 4 will go into depth about ebook publishing, one of the most popular and successful avenues for authors right now.

Case study: getting published

G. Michael Schneider is the perfect example of an author who took his knowledge turned it into a how-to travel book called *On the Other's Guy's Dime* (2010). How did writing this book come about?

'When I retired from teaching in 2007, my children (daughter Rebecca, son Benjamin, son-in-law Trevor) gave me a ten-week travel writing class at the Gotham Writers Workshop in NYC as a retirement gift. They thought it would be a wonderful idea for me to write a memoir about the places my wife and I have lived and worked over our 30 year professional career. I agreed to attend the class, although I felt the best I could hope for is something the children and grandchildren might read to learn about where Mom and Dad, Grandma and Grandpa have been. I didn't expect anyone else to ever take a look. Well, the teacher, Mr. Kurt Oprecht, was an extremely inspiring instructor, and when I told him about my ideas he convinced me to raise expectations about who might be interested in learning how to travel as we did —short-term postings that pay enough to cover your expenses. He inspired me to produce a book that would be of interest to a wider audience than just my immediate family. Fifteen months after completing that class I finished the first draft of On The Other Guys Dime.

What was the most challenging and rewarding things about writing a book?

By far, the most rewarding thing is receiving email, blog comments, and tweets from people who have read the book and are determined to create similar experiences for themselves and their family. For example: "My husband and I love to travel internationally and your blog on working overseas has definitely piqued our interest."; "I will have a sabbatical within one or two years. I would like to work abroad and will benefit from reading your book to learn how to do it."

It bothers me when people say how "lucky" I am to have lived and worked overseas more than a dozen times. No, I am not lucky. What I am is fully committed to doing whatever is necessary to create these exotic, no-cost travel experiences. I am not some special, well-connected, influential bigwig, but rather a fairly average, college teacher at a small liberal arts school. Anyone who reads the book and has the same type of commitment can be just as lucky.

It can be difficult to break into the "big time," that is, to find a major publishing house that will print and distribute your book. So the great majority of travel writers will never see the kind of sales achieved by someone like a Bill Bryson or Paul Theroux. However, if you approach your writing projects with realistic expectations you can have a great deal of personal success.

For example, if you cannot attract a major publisher, consider self-publishing. Start your own travel blog and hope it catches the eye of a wide audience. Write short travel articles for magazines such as Conde Nast, Travel + Leisure, Budget Travel, or airline in-flight magazines. Submit articles to popular travel ezines, such as Romar Traveler. Just as the music industry has undergone a massive upheaval, so has the publishing business. Today, there are a lot of outlets for good travel writing and you really should consider all of them as potential destinations for your stories.'

Fiction vs non-fiction

NON-FICTION

Non-fiction relies solely on the truth which means being factually correct is imperative. Travel writers relying on personal experience have to be careful not to embellish their stories with events that didn't happen or incorrect details. This is where good writing comes into play. Non-fiction writers must also channel their sleuth skills since many non-fiction articles use sources as the foundation of an article.

FICTION

Fiction is for pure enjoyment. The story is developed from the writer's imagination and can cover a number of genres. Well travelled writers can use their experiences by recalling images, colours, scents, tastes and sounds to bring their stories to life (see the case study below about airline captain Henry Biernacki).

Remember this

Before you start writing, think about whether you have a story worth telling. The more extraordinary the story and writing, the more successful you will be. A unique angle is everything in travel writing.

Case study: fiction travel writing

Henry Biernacki 'Global Henry' (http://TheGlobalHenry.com) has travelled to over 120 countries. His latest book is *No More Heroes* (2010). He has the following advice:

Extend yourself and learn by taking public transit anywhere you go, ask everyone questions, get lost in the confusion of a new city, and ultimately most of your day is consumed without spending money, but modestly gathering experiences. That is the reason why we travel: to grasp hold of the newness in a nation where people are going to offer you to sit, visit, and finally may request you to meet their entire family. The only important part of any trip to a destination is the entire process of going through a country.

Carry more books than clothes, which is admirable, since you are going to be in need of words, describing a situation, then you can sell the books to the guesthouse. Travel with things you do not mind getting stolen. Assume anything you have will be stolen. You are going to be distracted, lost, and trying to find your way around a capital. You are going to be asking a lot of questions and touts can sense who is lost. Travel with a medium size rucksack. You will not be tempted to buy anything. Be sure to take a few Ziploc bags to keep your things dry.

Many people arrive at a destination to research their topic when research is in the travel itself. Tourists have a destination. That is why there is always somewhere to go for a tourist always paying for something else. A traveller knows that the somewhere does not matter and somewhere can catch up anytime, knowing a story is being cultivated.

The test of one's character is not doing something, an action, which you know you can perform; but rather having the sureness of undertaking something of which you are wholly naïve and still making it all work in your favour.

Do I need an agent?

Signing with a literary agent is one of the most exciting things to happen to a writer. For one thing, it validates the writer. It means that someone else not only sees the writer's talent, but that someone is going to stand up for the writer and help propel their career.

Seeking a literary agent can be a long and gruelling process and isn't something a new travel writer should worry about until they have been published for a while or if they have already written a book that is ready to be presented to publishers.

Unless you have an extraordinary story to tell, it's best to start from the ground and work your way up, building your platform, collecting clips and learning your way around the travel writing world.

In addition to writing well, burgeoning writers need to have a solid platform. See Chapter 13 for more about platforms and self-branding.

If you are convinced you're ready for an agent, browse http://AgentQuery.com or http://QueryTracker.net to find literary agents.

Case study: Travel writing tips

Chuck Sambuchino is the editor of the *Writer's Digest Books Guide to Literary Agents* and *Children's Writer's and Illustrator's Market*. He is also the author of the writing books *Formatting and Submitting Your Manuscript*

(2009) as well as *Create A Writer Platform* (2012). He is a popular presenter at writers' conferences and runs the Guide to Literary Agents Blog (guidetoliteraryagents.com/blog), one of the biggest blogs in publishing.

> The best way to break into travel writing, in my mind, is to start with a trip you're already taking. Examine a business trip or vacation you'll take during the next year that's in an interesting location. Do some online research of the location and talk to a few locals there who can point you to interesting entertainment and nightlife sites/sights. Use all this info and query a magazine for an instalment to their recurring travel section. When you pitch the publication, try to stress that your feature will include a mix of old and new ideas for what to do in (the location). Also state your flexibility in the matter, in case the editor has a different idea about what to write about in the piece.

> Magazines are much more likely to say yes to a travel article – especially if the writer is new – if the writer asks them to reimburse few/no travel expenses. If you're having trouble, don't forget to try and pitch local, smaller magazines that are much more open to working with local/newer writers. If you shoot for a large magazine (such as one found on airplanes), don't be surprised if they say no. They get tons of query ideas every week – most from writers with more experience than you.

> If you get the assignment, add 1–2 days to the proposed trip so you can investigate locations personally. This will help you meet interesting people and describe locations firsthand. The trip extension shouldn't affect your plane fare, but it will affect your hotel and food costs. Try to offset these increases by telling people you're writing a travel article. For example, call up several of the area's nicer hotels and explain to their public relations contact about your article – then inquire about a 'media rate' (i.e., a discounted, or possibly free, rate in exchange for writing about your stay at the hotel, which, logically, should be quite nice). You will get a variety of responses, but at least one hotel, if not several, should offer a discount room for you. Restaurants are likely to give you a free or discounted meal if you say upfront how you're mentioning them in a decent-sized publication. You'll still be a little in the hole concerning overall costs, but you'll get back in the black after receiving the check for the article.

Other writing outlets

NON-PROFIT ORGANIZATIONS

Some writers will contribute their writing to non-profit organizations. Before you offer to contribute out of the goodness of your heart, ask if there is any room in their budget for some type of compensation. Many non-profit organizations put aside money for such cases. In this business it never hurts to ask.

NON-TRAVEL ASSIGNMENTS

If your ultimate goal is to work full-time as a freelance travel writer, consider taking on non-travel writing assignments. These can help supplement your income between travel assignments. Depending on your situation, there will be times of the year when you won't be travelling. For example, if you're a parent the end of the school year can be tough for travelling.

Press trips vary from season to season and are rarely offered over the holidays. Having extra work to fall back on can only help.

Seattle-based travel writer and blogger Pam Mandel of NerdsEyeView.com is an example of someone who has a thriving business as a freelance technical writer/copy writer/content strategist but also works as an admired travel writer:

> *I work on projects that run from a few hours of editing to a few months of working as part of a web design and development team. Candidly, I can't imagine how I'd get by without this work. The bulk of our household income comes from my technical project earnings – it's how we pay for our mortgage, our health insurance, just about everything.*

I'm not sure I'd have it any other way. The fact that I am able to earn a good living outside of travel writing allows me to do some interesting things. It allows me to take off big chunks of time to travel and write. It allows me to be really selective about the markets I pursue – I'm not trying to publish everywhere, all the time. And it allows me to focus on doing the kind of travel writing I love – creative narrative – rather than continually chasing down the absolutely more lucrative and marketable service pieces.'

Try it now

Use any of your writing that has been published to your advantage, even if your clips are not travel-related. Scoring a byline on any topic can help you transition into travel writing. If you have published articles, pull them out, dust them off and put them to work.

Remember this

There is a poster in the hallway of my children's school. The photo shows a toddler stacking blocks and the phrase on the poster states, 'Every expert was once a beginner'.

Think of yourself as that child stacking the blocks, only you are not using blocks, you are using words. With every word you type you are creating something remarkable. Start now.

Focus points

Identify the type of writing you wish to pursue.

Know your article's purpose.

Start with what you know then grow from there.

Looking for stories close to home is an easy way to break into travel writing

Look for opportunities in non-travel publications.

Next step

Today's era of online opportunities, smartphones and electronics has launched a new sphere of outlets for travel writers including websites, blogs, electronic applications and ebooks.

4

Online and Non-Traditional Opportunities

In this chapter you will learn:

- ▶ *Important factors in online travel writing*
- ▶ *Where to look for assignments*
- ▶ *About ebook publishing*
- ▶ *About apps and digital magazines*

Websites, blogs and self-publishing

Don't let the glamour of running your own website fool you. Producing a high-quality site or blog takes a lot of time as well as a financial investment.

It's true, there are plenty of high-quality blogs and websites out there with top-notch content that skip the bells and whistles, but if you're wishing for a glossy site with cool features expect to dish out the cash.

SPECIALIZATION IS ESSENTIAL ONLINE

Throughout this book the constant theme is about the importance of using your knowledge and expertise to develop your travel writing career; this advice is even more relevant when it comes to the online world.

'I think it's almost imperative to be a specialist these days,' says respected author and travel writer Durant Imboden. 'The Web is a niche medium, and the best way to stand out from the thousands or millions of other travel sites and blogs is to be an expert on a specific topic – which can be a destination, an activity like skiing or horseback riding, an age group (children's travel, teen educational travel, senior travel) or something else.'

THE BENEFITS OF SELF-PUBLISHING ONLINE

Self-publishing online will mean that unless you hire someone or have a partner, you are running the show 24 hours a day, 7 days a week. As with any business, there are pros and cons, but as long as you're web savvy the benefits will likely outweigh the cons.

▶ **Benefits**

▶ You keep the income.

▶ You set your own hours and deadlines.

▶ You'll be recognized as an expert, assuming you are publishing quality content.

If you're trying to decide whether to jump in and launch a website or test the waters by writing for other online publications, Imboden offers some good advice from both sides of the fence:

> Someone who's never worked in journalism or publishing can learn a lot by working with professionals who have. On the other hand, it's hard to find paying gigs if you don't have experience, and the cost of becoming a web publisher is low, so there's something to be said for learning by doing – even if it means making mistakes along the way.

> 'New travel writers have so many more options than when I started in magazines in the 1980s,' says Travel + Leisure editor Mark Orwoll. 'Back then it was print or nothing. Nowadays writers can build their following, promote themselves, and, in some cases, earn actual money, through websites, personal blogs, ebooks, iPad apps, and mobile phone apps.'

Remember this

If you have a job that allows for flexible days off, you may want to continue working for the benefits while enjoying the perks of owning your own travel blog or website. Shannon Hurst Lane of TravelingMamas. com balances a career with running her own website. She says, 'Being a website owner gives me an outlet for my true passion while working a full time job to support my family. It keeps me happy and sane.'

MORE THAN WRITING

If you are interested in taking advantage of the online travel market, you could consider launching a travel-planning site (as opposed to freelance or publishing a blog). Durant Imboden offers helpful information at TravelWritten.com and he recommends Tom Brosnahan's WritersWebsitePlanner.com.

TEAM WITH LIKE-MINDED BUSINESSES

Corporations today are joining forces with writers and bloggers to maintain current information on their websites. For example,

Expedia.com a large international travel planning site has teamed up with travellers who write blogs and record video to promote their business. These partnerships are a win-win for both the contributors and the company.

Try it now

Introduce yourself to any travel-minded businesses or publication (hotels, restaurants, attractions, your local tourism board, newspapers) that are lacking a blog presence. Include three things in your letter.

* who you are
* what you specialize in
* why they can benefit from your contribution.

At the close, offer to send examples of posts you can write. Tailor the piece to the publication and their market. For example, if the hotel brand you're approaching caters to business travellers, write a post about dry cleaning or how to find business centres while on the road.

Case study: An editor's point of view

Tim Leffel is author of four travel books including *Travel Writing 2.0: Earning money from your travels in the new media landscape* (2010), winner of multiple 'best travel writing' awards, and editor of several publications, including the narrative webzine PerceptiveTravel.com.

'Print magazines won't go away and books won't go away: they're just morphing a bit. At the same time the number of online outlets open to freelancers continues to grow.

There's a trade-off between the short- and long-term that's inherent in this job. Long-term, you need to be building up something you own yourself and getting a tribe of followers that cares what you have to say. That's the only way you're going to be able to make real money from this endeavor in the future outside of staff positions at publications. In the short term, however, the best bet is to hustle hard to get assignments and combine multiple streams of income from different sources: print, one-off online articles, regular blogging gigs, and whatever else you can scrape together. Online is much easier to break into and is a growing market, whereas print is shrinking. There's less money in online writing, but a lot more opportunity. Just evaluate the options well as some are pure scams.

Know your stuff...

Like most editors, I'm looking for signs that the writer knows Perceptive Travel well and has a firm grasp on what we do and do not publish. I also want to see that they have read the guidelines. I'd say 90 per cent don't make it past those first two filters. After that, I want to see a history of great narrative writing and credentials that will give me confidence they won't make me spend hours on editing and rewrites. I'm looking for signs the writer knows what a good story is, that they can do more than talk about their own thoughts and the destination. We're not a site for beginners I'm afraid. All our writers have lots of experience before they show up in this webzine.

For the blogs I edit, I'm looking for writers who can come up with something interesting to say on a weekly basis and are dependable. Professionalism matters more than panache in a blogging job. Post on time, take good photos, format things correctly, and get the right keywords in there. I've got no patience for laziness. You have to be an interesting writer, sure, but it's not like writing for the Atlantic or Smithsonian. A blog is much more conversational and you can push the conventional boundaries lot more, but keeping to your commitments and minding the techie details matter a lot.'

ONLINE TO PRINT

In some cases online work leads to print opportunities, but sometimes there's no need to go anywhere, as travel writer Rolf Potts explains:

> 'I got started in the late 1990s, and I was one of the first travel writers to begin his career online and move into print from there (instead of the other way around). These days you'll find travel writers who start out online and have no particular ambition to move into print, since the print market is shrinking. There are both advantages and disadvantages to the shrinking of the print market. One disadvantage is that pay rates are pretty miserable; the per-word fees for a given travel story haven't changed much in 30 years – and when those rates have changed,

they've tended to go down. An advantage of the diminished influence of print is that it has been replaced by a much more diverse (and often more chaotic) online market. This hasn't helped pay rates any, but it gives beginning writers a much wider writing market to break into.'

Print to online

Writers who started out as freelance writers for print publications have slowly been making the transition to online writing and Donna Hull is one such writer:

> *'Originally, all of my freelance writing assignments involved print publications. Around 2008, those publications began dying off, so I transferred all of my efforts to online writing. It's the best career decision that I've ever made. Besides writing for online markets, I also publish a blog, MyItchyTravelFeet.com, the baby boomer's guide to travel, which guarantees coverage from the trips that I take.'*

Durant Imboden impressed the globe with his online success as publisher of Europeforvisitors.com. Imboden's writing career has progressed over time and has included stints as a magazine writer and book author. He has also freelanced for ad agencies, written destination brochures and edited the Northwest Airlines 'WorldPerks Senior Traveler' newsletter:

> *'In 1996, I created a website titled 'The Baby Boomer's Venice' as a test project for a magazine review of Microsoft Front Page 1.1. The next year, I started writing about Venice and Europe for About.com (then called The Mining Co.). My wife was the MiningCo/About.com 'Guide' for Switzerland and Austria. We parted ways with About. com in fall of 2001 and launched Europeforvisitors.com a month later. I haven't freelanced in about ten years.'*

As they say, the rest is history. The couple has now made the website their full-time job.

For writers wondering whether to approach established publications or test the waters with their own site, Imboden believes there's pros and cons to both:

Someone who's never worked in journalism or publishing can learn a lot by working with professionals who have. On the other hand, it's hard to find paying gigs if you don't have experience, and the cost of becoming a web publisher is low, so there's something to be said for learning by doing – even if it means making mistakes along the way.

Online travel guides

Online travel guides have been slowly swallowing the number of print guidebooks, though I do still see tourists reading print guidebooks on the plane. For many years I've been contributing to various online guides; some have my byline while others do not. The one thing I've learned over the years is that information can get dated quickly. Look at this as an opportunity for work.

Try it now

Visit your favourite online travel guide(s) and see if any information needs to be updated. Once you've discovered an area that could use a facelift, take notes on the outdated material, contact the editor and ask if they would be interested in your services for revising the content.

Content farms

Content farms are websites that employ scores of freelance writers to produce articles for the site. About.com and Examiner.com are two examples. The writers specialize in one or more topics and are paid based on the number of page views the articles receive. Some topics naturally draw high page views while other topics, the more specialized niches, don't see as many hits. Personally, I've never contributed to such sites, but I know many writers who have. Some have been disappointed in the low pay their personal topic produces while others feel that it has helped elevate their 'expert' status.

Freelance travel writer Diana Rowe (http://DianaRowe.com and http://travellinginheels.com) has written for Examiner.com as the Denver Travel Examiner since December 2008; she sees a steady flow of visitors:

> When I began writing for Examiner.com, it was a conscious decision to get my 'name' out there more as the cash pay-off is usually negligible. Posts to your Examiner title are short, a little longer than blog posts – 400 words or so – but it's really about adding another outlet for your writing. Since I travel to so many places (from Israel to South America to the US, and places between), I feel it's important to share my travels with my readers, and at the same time, offer my hosts more publicity. I often rewrite an excerpt of a longer article, focusing on one aspect of the travel. For example, I took a Quebec City feature for a business publication, excerpted my experience at the Ice Hotel (Hôtel de Glace) and posted a 'room report'. Of course, some Examiners do well (and again that's relative), but they also are nearly daily (or more) contributors to their 'title'. Bottom line? Examiner.com is an outlet to keep your name visible online and add more depth and content to your travels.

New expectations

As a participant in the new travel writing era, a travel writer is expected to do more than write an article, meet the deadline and send an invoice. Writers are also expected to provide photos, images, videos to accompany our work, write with SEO (search engine optimization) in mind and often promote content via social media.

For example, a website that I have been contributing for a few years monitors the traffic of each writer's work and those whose articles draw the most views are more likely to score assignments down the road as well as pay increases. Some online publications do expect writers to use their social media clout to bring readers to their articles because high visitor numbers means higher advertising revenue. When the writers succeed, the publications are more likely to increase writer pay. In other words, when writing online the numbers matter.

Mistakes corrected

Before you publish online, be sure to read over your work. Fortunately, online articles can be corrected if a typo sneaks though. I recall submitting an article to an online publication and within in a few days the editor wrote to tell me the piece was live. I clicked on the link and was mortified. The article was riddled with typos and appeared unfinished. I had no idea what happened to the piece I had worked so hard on. It ended up that I had accidentally sent an earlier, back-up version, instead of the final article. Obviously, the piece was never read before being posted. I emailed the editor immediately with apologies as well as the correct version. The two lessons I learned from that experience are:

1 Always verify you're sending the correct, edited version. Write 'final' in the file name.

2 Always read your online work when published so revisions can be made immediately if necessary.

Remember this

'Determination and hard work are the key to success, especially for travel writers. It can be very difficult at the beginning when you're faced with constant rejection, but once you get your first commission, it'll be a much smoother ride from there onwards. There's nothing more fulfilling than living your dream.'

Nellie Huang, travel writer and editor-in-chief of www.wildjunket.com, an award-winning travel blog focusing on outdoor adventures and travel.

Electronic books (ebooks)

Print, online and blogging are all fine and dandy travel writing choices, but if you really want to step it up a notch and become immersed in the electronic era, ebooks are becoming popular with writers of all genres and their readers. Having the opportunity to carry as many books as a reader wishes on a Nook, Kindle or tablet has made travelling with books more convenient. Today, most print books come in an ebook edition, and some publishers are producing ebook only titles. ebooks pay similar to print books with an advance and royalties.

Furthermore, ebooks offer opportunities for self-publishing. Writers don't have to sign with a publisher in order to write and produce their own ebook, which means they have more control over the direction of their career and the profits.

Angela England (angcngland.com) caught on to the benefits of writing ebooks when she grouped a series of her blog posts together for her readers in an ebooklet. Her first large ebook *Making Money From Your Blogging in New Ways* was published in 2009. 'The ebook sales, and clients generated through having published the ebook, added five figures to my family's income through 2010,' she says. In addition she has written *30 Days to Make and Sell a Fabulous Ebook* (30dayebook.com).

She shares with writers the five things to keep in mind as they create their eBook:

1 *Select a topic carefully. Topic selection is so vital to an ebook's overall success that I spend two full days covering this in the workbook. You want to choose a topic that is not so broad you can't compete, but not so narrow you have no potential audience. Find that sweet spot of focused, interesting and saleable topics and you're in a good place!*

2 *Be professional. That means having professional cover art, images, formatting or editing for your ebook. You may need to invest some money to hire help in areas where you aren't skilled.*

3 *Begin creating buzz for your ebook before the book launches. Don't be afraid to announce the coming arrival of your book. Working up against a deadline might keep you motivated, and knowing that others are getting excited about your coming work is exciting.*

4 *Take advantage of new technologies. My first ebooks weren't available on digital readers – they didn't exist. With Kindle and Nook and even smart phones capable of taking ebooks on the go, be sure you provide your ebook in a variety of formats.*

5   *Enlist the help of others. One of the best things I did was to allow others to sign up as affiliates to sell my ebook on my behalf. When someone sells my ebook, they get a portion of the revenues and in exchange, my work is introduced to people who wouldn't have otherwise seen it.*

'Creating an ebook can be difficult, but so beneficial at the same time,' says England. 'Done correctly, it can give a blogger greater credibility, an additional stream of revenue, and spread the message you're passionate about to an entirely new audience.'

Case study: ebook publishing

Dana Lynn Smith, The Savvy Book Marketer, (TheSavvyBookMarketer. com and SavvyEbookPublishing.com) draws on her 17 years of publishing experience to help authors learn how to sell more books through her how-to guides, training programs, coaching, blog, and newsletter:

▶ Platforms

Amazon's Kindle is the most important ebook platform. Whether you create your own ebook file or hire someone to do it, I recommend setting up your own account on Amazon's Kindle Direct Publishing platform rather than going through an ebook publishing service. This will give you full control of your Kindle publishing account and your payments will come directly from Amazon.

While the majority of ebook sales still come from the Kindle store, Barnes & Noble's Nook store and Apple's iBookstore are gaining market share due to the popularity of the Nook tablets and the iPad. However, many iPad owners buy their ebooks from the Kindle store rather than Apple's iBookstore because Amazon offers a superior shopping experience.

If you don't want to spend time setting up accounts directly on other ebookstores like Barnes & Noble and Apple, you can publish to those platforms and others through an aggregator such as Smashwords.com.

To learn how to create and publish ebooks, see the Ebook Publishing Success program, available at http://bit.ly/EbookPubSuccess or www.SavvyEbookPublishing.com.

▶ Promoting ebooks

Ebooks are promoted in much the same ways as printed books, but there are some additional things you can do to boost ebook sales. Here are some tips for promoting Kindle books:

✳ Make sure the print book and ebook edition are linked together on the Amazon website.

✳ Include a link to your Kindle version from your own website, and remind people that they don't have to own a Kindle device to read Kindle books. Customers can read Kindle books by using the Kindle app on various devices including computers, tablets and cell phones. The phone app could be a big selling point for travel guides, since it makes your book easily portable. You can even point customers to http://amzn.to/GetKindleApp where they can download the Kindle app.

✳ Keywords are important to helping shoppers discover non-fiction books on Amazon. Include keywords in your book's title and/or subtitle and add keyword "tags" to your book directly from the book's sales page on Amazon.com. When publishing your ebook on the Kindle Direct Publishing platform, be sure to choose appropriate categories and keywords.

✳ Make sure your ebook is priced competitively and your sales copy is compelling and contains quotes from your best reviews.

✳ Consider using KDP Select to promote your Kindle books.

✳ Learn more about promoting books and ebooks at www.TheSavvyBookMarketer.com.

▶ Pricing

Ebook buyers are very price sensitive and they expect ebooks to cost much less than printed books. In general, customers will pay more for a non-fiction ebook on a topic that they need to know about than they will for fiction, which is bought for entertainment. A price between $4.99 and $8.99 (£3.20 and £5.75) is probably a good range for travel books, but be sure to consider the price of competing books. If your ebook is short, you may need to price it lower.

Kindle pays a 70% royalty for books priced between $2.99 and $9.99 (£1.90 and £6.40) and 30% for other price points. Keep in mind that you can experiment with different price points.

Electronic applications (apps)

The travel app world is still a mystery to most travel writers. I have my list of favourite travel apps that I can't live without, but they're also an option for bringing in extra income.

Author and freelance journalist Kimberly Button (http://kimbutton.com) explains:

> *'Apps are a great market for travel writers, but you've got to be aware that they require constant updating. Because of the digital format, people expect what they access to be valid on that date, not the date when you wrote it (unlike a book). You've got to be willing to constantly be in the field for the topic that you're writing about if you want to make apps a part of your revenue.'*

Case study: apps

Minh Tran is founder and CEO of Cab Match (www.cabmatch.com). He has developed several iPhone and Android travel-themed apps, including http://savemytire.com and http://goteventz.com. He offers some insight and tips on getting started in this line of work.

Q: How does someone break into app development?

A: You will need a team of developers: graphics designer, iPhone/Android developer, and web developer with custom API background to develop code that will communicate from server to phone. If you don't have a strong computer background, it is better to hire an agency that already has a team of developers that create apps: http://TheyMakeApps.com and www.GetAppsDone.com.

Q: How do app developers market their work best?

A: Twitter and press coverage. LinkedIn is a good way to connect to influential people in your industry to perhaps endorse your product. Having a blog also helps and getting mentioned on other blogs as well. I have had lukewarm success with Facebook wall postings and advertising. However, it is still necessary to have a Facebook page for Google Search reasons. YouTube demo videos are a must.

Q: Do you have any tips for wishful app developers?

A: No app is perfect on first release. You will be making many revisions as development moves along. Keep your app as simple as possible with the least features on first release. It is important to note that the user interface is a very critical part of app making. You have to make it very simple to use with focus on guiding the user along each screen. Since you will be heavily into the project, you will know your product too well and it will be difficult to step back and see it in a new user's eyes. Have lots of people use your app. Also, before any coding even starts, make a paper story board and have your friends and family try to use your 'story board' paper version. When your story board is finalized, then you can bring it to the graphics designer/iPhone/android/web developer to begin development. This will save you a lot of money by doing this first. Any time you change anything, there will be a chance of introducing new bugs. Wait one month after your app is released before proposing the app to the press. The reason is that after you release your app, bugs will show up or you may make user interface changes once you see how people use your app. You will be surprised! I suggest buying books on app making. For your webpage, buy a template at http://themeforest.net for great looking websites on the cheap.

Q: Is the app world competitive and/or lucrative?

A: More competitive and less lucrative. It is like opening a pizza shop in Little Italy. You either need to have the best pizza or a lot of marketing. Creating an app is the easy part. Marketing it and convincing people to use it will be the bigger challenge.

Digital magazines

Nellie Huang, a professional travel journalist specializing in adventure travel and her photographer husband recently launched the 100-page *WildJunket* magazine, a digital flipbook magazine covering offbeat destinations, outdoorsy activities, unusual corners of the world, special interest journeys and deep cultural experiences ranging from engaging narrative accounts to photo essays to short dispatches and food articles – many of them contributed by talented and acclaimed travel writers from around the world. Huang explains:

> 'As you can imagine, creating the magazine involved a lot of hard work, time and effort. I had to pick up several new skills as an editor and my husband also worked day and night on the design of the magazine. We've been very lucky to have several writers help contribute and edit pieces. But now looking at the final product, the hard work's well worth it and we can't wait to see what the future of the magazine has in store for us. The bi-monthly digital magazine is available for purchase on our magazine retail partners, Zinio and Magzter.'

Focus points

Don't limit your travel writing opportunities to print publications.

Approach websites that may be lacking in certain areas and show the editor you are capable of producing appropriate content for their site.

If you're not having any luck landing your work with a traditional publisher, consider self-publishing an ebook.

Experiment with apps, you may find your have a knack for it.

If you've always dreamt about having your own magazine, make it happen with an online issue.

Next step

Travel writing can't happen without experience and research. Chapter 5 is going to assist you in how to perform proper research as well as be your guide to landing media invitations and tell you what to do before, during and after your trips.

Research and the Press Trip

In this chapter you will learn:

▶ *About the phases of researching for travel writing*

▶ *What resources are available for research*

▶ *About press trips: how to get invited and how they work*

Now it's time for things to get exciting. In this chapter we will look at two important aspects of travel writing: travel and research.

The importance of research

Before you approach an editor or even begin to write a query letter, research must be conducted to back up your article. Fact-checking should be done before, during and after your travels. Editor Chris Anderson of Huffington Post describes the process:

> 'There are two ways many writers approach travelling and travel writing. One, just picking a place, going in blind and hoping what you discover ends up being amazing and worth writing about. Two, doing lots of research about a place, contacting people ahead of time and setting up an itinerary. Personally, I prefer a mix of the two. Plan ahead by connecting with interesting locals and people who know the city and, more importantly, people who can introduce you to interesting characters and places. But leave time to take that right turn and do some wandering. The delight of travel is discovery, and you need to be able to relate that to your readers. If you can't do that, you can't be a travel writer.'

If you wish to write a story about a place you've already visited, or plan to visit, it's imperative to check the website to make sure the information is still current. Call to verify that any hotels, restaurants or attractions are still open. Verify statistics and figures. For example, what is the best time of year to visit Peru? Is Park City's Alpine Slide open year-round? Save yourself the embarrassment of being told a venue that you are planning to write about is closed due to a hurricane or fire. Chris Anderson has more advice on this:

> 'Make sure the information you provide is correct. Double-check the address, phone number, opening hours, and anything else relevant to somebody that is going to read your article and follow in your footsteps. Because they will, and if you send them to some dark alley somewhere and they get lost or mugged, your editor might get a call

and you might never work for them again. Always, always remember that if you're giving recommendations you have to have accurate info. Always think about the 'getting there' portion of your story. You want to share your experiences, so make sure that those who follow your lead can do so with ease.'

Remember this

Following the latest travel trend can enhance your travel writing career and make your work attractive to publications. Editors like to stay on top of the latest and greatest, so if you can offer insight into what's hip, or about to be, you will naturally become the go-to writer. Follow companies like PhoCusWright.com, read travel blogs, attend travel and tourism conferences and check in on Google trends regularly (google.com/trends/) by plugging in 'travel' to reveal the most popular destination requests.

The trends aren't always destination based. Sometimes they're themes such as girlfriend getaways and babymoons. If the subject is relevant and upcoming editors want to hear about it. Of course, some topics are already on the editor's desk like the winter or summer Olympics, local festivals and events. The key, once again, is to find a particular angle that stands out.

What is a press trip?

Let's start with the basics. Behind-the-scenes public relations people have a bevy of clients wishing to get exposure for their business or destination. The PR personnel work with the hotels, restaurants and attractions to coordinate a multi-day tour that allows the writers a chance to experience what the business and destination offers. From the writer's perspective, the planned itinerary allows for a planned, low-cost experience and the opportunity to find unique angles as well as observe what's hot in that region or what's classic.

Press trip planners need to protect their clients by ensuring the planned trip will pay off. One way they do this is to ask writers to provide a letter of assignment from the publication that has accepted the story. This is where your pre-trip query comes in. In other words, you approach an editor with your story idea before you take the trip. The other approach is to invite writers who have proved they can land assignments, with the expectation they will successfully pitch their stories after the trip.

TYPES OF PRESS TRIP

Press trips were once reserved for writers on assignment for top-tier publications, but that's changed. The new press trip includes writers from various formats, including trips designed for bloggers.

Press trips come in all shapes and sizes and are tailored to different needs. Just as there are a variety of types of travel writers, there are also various types of press trips. Some trips are generic, appealing to a variety of writers, whereas others involve planned itineraries designed to spotlight specific areas.

The traditional press trip normally consists of an assortment of travel writers or editors who write for diverse publications. These trips are usually designed to be a one-size-fits-all with a general theme such as arts, antiques, weddings, culinary or adventure.

Group press trips

It's unlikely that more than one person will be representing the same publication during a press trip unless it is a group blogging trip. As the owner of a shared blog, my co-writers and I frequently get invitations for the three of us to travel together. During such trips we are expected to blog repeatedly about our experience. We cover the accommodation, restaurants, activities and any other note-worthy items we come across. However, we're also expected to land assignments with our other print and online outlets. Because each of us are established in our field, the trips we have done have easily produced multiple stories for each of us.

▶ Individual press trip

When you have a specific niche or are writing a very specific article, the individual press trip is the ideal way to get your topic covered without having to worry about wasting your time on activities that don't pertain to you. PR people from tourism boards and convention and visitors bureaus are most helpful and are always willing to accommodate you if you can prove you are working on a specific article. Sometimes a PR representative will offer to accompany you on your tours and explorations or they may ask if you prefer to be on your own.

A benefit to travelling solo, rather than with a group or guide, is having an authentic experience. There is no one to translate for you, answer your questions or ensure you make it to your next appointment on time. Therefore, be prepared to research your area before going, study maps, take cash for tipping drivers, guides, locals who allow you to take their photograph or any other person who deserves to be compensated for their time and knowledge, and learn the customs of the region. In addition, learn key phrases that may come in handy, and take a phrasebook or download a language phone app for better communication. Showing you are making an effort to learn the native language goes a long way.

▶ Twitter trips

Some companies have been jumping on the Twitter wagon by inviting writers to attend Twitter trips. These tours are press trips, but the focus is to Tweet and post photos about your experiences on Twitter. Followers can watch your progress by plugging in the trip's designated hashtag (#followed by a keyword, phrase or acronym). For example, the Princess Cruises Alaska Cruisetour Twitter Trip I went on with my mum and ten other travel writers, bloggers and photographers attached the hashtag #FollowMeAtSea to our Tweets. The benefit for me was not only the amazing experience but also fodder and photographs for article ideas.

▶ Specialized press trips

These are trips that are designed to entertain niche writers. For example, if the writers cover weddings or honeymoons the trip will focus on ceremony locations, resort tours, romantic amenities and wine tastings. An adventure-themed trip will include non-stop action. Think parasailing, scubadiving and skydiving. Whereas a 'soft' adventure trip may include kayaking, snorkelling or a casual bike tour.

▶ Family trips

Family press trips do exist, but there are some things you should know about them. First of all, sometimes despite the 'family press trip' title, only the journalist is invited. When children are invited, this is usually just the writer and one child (normally this includes air travel). However, it never hurts to ask if you can pay for your other child/children's way if there's room.

If the sponsor declines your offer, there is likely to be a reason such as there isn't enough room on the buses being used on the tour, or dinner reservations have a limited capacity. If this is a deal-kill, be gracious, thank your contact for the offer and ask to be kept in mind for future trips.

Why go on a press trip?

There are both advantages and disadvantages to attending a press trip. Naturally, the most attractive reason is travel. Experiencing once in a lifetime adventures on a regular basis has been the most exciting part of their new-found career, say Dave and Deb of PlanetD.com, 'Whenever we try something new, we have to pinch ourselves and can't believe that we are actually taking part in an adventure such as sailing to Antarctica, flying a stunt plane, climbing to Everest Base Camp or flying a helicopter over Alaskan glaciers. The opportunities that we have had were something that we could only dream of a few years ago.' Yet, you still need to understand the pros and cons of press trip travel:

▶ Benefits

▶ You will meet other travel writers.

▶ You will generate story ideas.

▶ You will see new places.

▶ You will meet professional guides who know the place you are visiting and want to write about.

▶ Press trips are fun!

▶ The itinerary is set for you – you don't have to plan your days.

► Negatives

► There will be pressure on you to land assignments.

► You will incur some costs (childcare, pet care, airfare) and these may outweigh the fee you earn from an assigned article.

► You may have to tour places that are not relevant to your assignment.

► You may not have an opportunity to see the town on your own.

► You might only see the city's tourist areas, rather than how the locals live.

► You may not be able to sell the article you write to the publication of your choice.

► The dreaded question ... May I bring a guest?

Some PR people cringe at this question. Extra people mean extra costs, but sometimes a plus-one is more than welcome and it is nice to get to experience a destination with someone you know. The general rule is if you plan to bring a spouse or friend, the airfare isn't included.

Also, don't try and bring along your spouse as your 'photographer' unless he or she really is a professional photographer. Today it's not hard to find out if someone is a professional and, yes, it's obvious if your companion is trying to 'scam'.

MANNERS

Following local customs, not comparing the trip to past trips to other destinations and common courtesy all add up to being a gracious guest. But that's not all. Even the way you perform your work, such as taking photos, can contribute to your being asked back or not. For example, Susan Farewell of FarewellTravels.com comments on food photography during press trips. 'It's okay to take photos of the various dishes you sample/eat on press trips, but think twice about the way in which you go about taking the photos. Should you be arranging things while a presentation is going on? Should you be moving chairs, place settings and possibly other diners? If you can take photos the way a doctor might give a child a vaccination – it's over before he/she knows it – fine. If you have to call attention to yourself in any way, don't do it.'

Remember this

Often press trips consist of sightseeing on a bus or in a van. If you're prone to car sickness inquire ahead of time whether there will be any vehicle tours and if so, ask to sit in the front and pack any medication you may need.

How to make the most of your press trip

Before packing your bags, preliminary research is important because you want to ensure you are getting the most of your time away from home and not wasting the time of the person working on your itinerary.

Putting on your Sherlock Holmes hat before you arrive at your destination will help you to have a foundation for your article. Dig for interesting tit-bits that may have never been revealed publicly before.

If you are part of a group trip, you may be expected to partake in activities that may not be relevant to your story. Handle such events graciously, but don't be too hasty – you may find a story worth reporting.

In all honesty, there's only one thing that matters when it comes to press trip invitations and that is good coverage. 'Coverage' is industry slang for being published. For print publications, that means how many readers the magazine or newspaper estimate. Traditionally, a feature story in a major newspaper scores a lot more points than a short piece in a small town paper. Online, this means an article in a top news site is preferred over a blog with minimal readers.

Social media savvy bloggers are expected to post on their website throughout the trip – that often means staying up late to write – but they also post live pictures and updates on their social media pages during their adventures. When all is said and done, bloggers writing for their own site don't benefit financially from their trip. But they do get the experience and the opportunity to add content to their personal site, which in turn will pull page views and result in attracting advertisers.

But, as you're about to discover, there are new tactics in play today that actually appeal to the whole range of writers and bloggers. PR firms are getting wise and realizing that, while some bloggers may not have the numbers of larger websites, their readers are a very specific niche that is a better market.

Remember this

Passport. Unless you have no interest in travelling internationally, run down to the nearest passport office and apply for a passport. The greatest press trip offer may come your way but without a passport you can't go anywhere.

Janet Groene, active member of Society of American Travel Writers (SATW), author of more than two dozen books, full-time freelance travel writer, author and columnist, offers a behind-the-scenes-peak at hosted trips:

'Press trips are perceived by some as 'free travel' but the only people who really travel free are salaried staffers who have an expense account. Their costs are covered by their publishers from the moment they leave home until they return. By contrast, freelance writers must pay for many things such as airport parking, getting to and from the airport, hotel incidentals, expenses while in transit and tips. Tips are often required and the amount specified. On cruise ships this can be in four figures. Many staffers do travel on press trips and their publication pays a press rate. The staffers themselves are still paying nothing out of pocket and they are 'on the clock' during the trip, receiving salary and benefits. Freelancers, on the other hand, are providing their time and effort in hopes of getting a fair return while at the same time maintaining all their own business expenses including health insurance, office expense, courses to keep up with technology, retirement and much more.'

Case study: press trips

Travel journalist Chris Gray Faust is a columnist at Frommers.com, a contributor to www.CruiseCritic.com and the former travel editor at *USA Today*. Her destination travel blog, Chris Around the World (http://caroundtheworld.com) won a Lowell Thomas Travel Writing award for blogging in 2010 and is syndicated on *USA Today* (http://travel.usatoday.com) as part of their Travel Alliance. A member of the Society of American Travel Writers, she's writing an ebook on using social media while travelling, and is the author of the *Philadelphia Essential Guide for iPhone and iPad* (2011). Besides working as a writer, she does social media consulting from her home in Seattle, where she lives with her husband, photography enthusiast Don Faust.

Chris has been on her share of press trips. Here's her take on one of her more recent excursions:

'Multi-course tasting menus. Five-star hotels. Free spa treatments. Sounds fabulous, right? Well, maybe. Forget lolling about on high-thread-count sheets: The life of a travel writer on a press trip is more about endurance than enjoyment.

Don't believe me? Take a gander at the first few days of a typical itinerary, from a press trip I took to Japan in early 2012.

Day One: Arrive in Osaka, Japan, after a 12-hour flight from Seattle. While the other people in my group have been able to fly directly to Hiroshima, I still have three hours and two trains to go before I reach my final destination. I'm met at baggage claim by a tour leader holding up a sign with my name on it. While she speaks English, she's worried about our tight connection, and taps her foot impatiently as I struggle to figure out the yen-to-dollar exchange rate at the ATM. I get cash and we're off on my first bullet train.

When we arrive at Hiroshima, the tour leader and I pile into a taxi. She's on the phone; apparently her boss is irritated because we're 30 minutes late to the official welcome dinner. 'Didn't he have my flight information?' I ask. She replies with a nod and eyeroll.

At the hotel, I have 15 minutes to check in before I need to get to the dinner. I race upstairs, jump into the shower and throw open my suitcase for a change of shirt. I blow dry my hair and apply makeup at the same time, bending down because the mirror is built at Japanese eye level. I grab my camera and iPhone, and make it downstairs with seconds to spare.

We walk to the dinner, where I greet my fellow press trip participants, three women whom I already know (this is rare; most press trips are made up of strangers thrown together from disparate media outlets). Our welcome dinner turns out to be a greasy Okonomiyaki savory pancake, served by an exuberant line cook who loves music videos. We journalists eat a few bites to satisfy our smiling hosts, even though the heavy taste is the last thing our jet-lagged stomachs crave. We're released back to the hotel at 10 pm, where I learn that most Japan hotels require broadband connections to use the Internet. I check my email after the staff delivers a cord I can use, and fall asleep around midnight.

Day Two: The alarm on my iPhone goes off at 6 am. I had been working on a blog post while I was on the plane and I review it carefully before hitting publish. I call my husband through Skype to let him know I made it safely. Then it's yet another record shower as I scramble to get ready and repack before breakfast (on this 12-day trip, we're in ten different hotels).

At breakfast, we're confronted by a Japanese buffet with food that has little resemblance to what you'd find at home. Boiled vegetables, salad and miso soup are surprisingly tasty. We're catching up when our tour leader rushes into the dining room. If we don't leave at 8 am, she says, our whole day will be messed up.

Our first stop is the Hiroshima Peace Memorial Museum. Despite our protests, we're told we only have 90 minutes to see this poignant marker of the A bomb damage. Yet our time on site is taken up by prefecture officials, who hand out business cards and read proclamations, and a film crew, who wants to document our visit (we're the first group of American journalists to visit Hiroshima since the March 11 earthquake and tsunami in northern Japan). We've also suffered an injury as one of the women on the trip, a photographer, slipped on the ice and crunched her hand on the way down. She'll have to visit the hospital later in the day.

I walk through the museum, snapping photos and trying to get enough alone time to absorb its message. All too soon, we're herded out to the Ota River, where we board a water taxi that will take us to Miyajima, a scenic island about 45 minutes away. Total time in Hiroshima since I've arrived in Japan: Less than 18 hours.

At Miyajima, we're immediately greeted by the island's tame deer, which ate my brochures. I laugh, as I don't want them anyway; my tour leader looks ready to kill me. She shoos me down the street toward lunch, where we indulge in oysters, the island's specialty.

After lunch, we head to the Itsukushima Shrine, a UNESCO World Heritage site. Its Torii (gate) is well-known from photos, but the light is wrong when we arrive. No matter, we tour the shrine, learning about Shinto New Year customs and vow to come back when the clouds are gone. Unbeknownst to us, our tour leaders have scheduled a hike to the Mount Misen cable car, an uphill activity that makes the TV producer on our trip quite unhappy (hey, you try hauling a heavy video camera up a mountain).

We take the two cable cars to the top of Mount Misen, but we're informed that we don't have enough time to visit the temples that are up there. That's OK, as the sun is finally out, making it possible to shoot the Torii in better light. Our tour leaders act like we're wasting time, but we stay at the gate for an hour or so, making sure that everyone has the shots that they need.

Our guide offers to take us to another temple, but I am done. I part from the group and head to the ryokan, a traditional Japanese inn, so I can check out the hot baths that I've heard so much about. I spend an hour soaking in a bath that gives me a great view of the sun setting over the Hiroshima Bay. This is the first relaxing moment I've had so far and it feels great.

Relaxation goes away when we gather for our first kaiseki, a multi-course Japanese feast that's full of pretty presentations and food that tastes nothing like it does in a sushi restaurant back home. Think tofu balls, taro cakes, fat-covered duck and other delicacies that seem bizarre to an American palate. We all perk up when rice is served toward the end.

A ryokan has shared rooms, and my roommate is snoring on her futon when I enter the room. I've scheduled a massage, which I'll pay from my own pocket, as it sounded good when the other journalists suggested it. Little did I know that most ryokans only provide Shiatsu massage, which involves pain before pleasure. Still, I'm exhausted and I quickly fall asleep, my muscles pounded into submission. Total time that I'll spend in Miyajima: Less than 24 hours.

And so it goes, for 12 full days (the schedule did ease up once we left the southern prefectures). While I wouldn't trade my time on the road for another job, it does take patience, stamina and just a bit of wheedling to make a press trip work. You need to be vigilant about how the itinerary will work for your audience, and seek out the angles that you know will resonate with your outlets. Otherwise, your experience will be an exhausting waste of time.'

MEDIA DISCOUNTS

Some writers and journalist prefer not to partake in group trips. There are many reasons for this. Sometimes tourism boards will connect writers with hotels, attractions, and restaurants who are willing to host or offer a discount to the writer. The assumption is that the writer will provide exposure by including the business in their story.

AIRLINE MILES

The fantastic thing about airline miles is that the flyer is the only one who can claim them. If a PR company is paying for your miles, be sure to submit your frequent flyer number to the booking agent or the airline before travelling. In fact, signup for airlines' reward programmes now so you have your number on hand when the time comes.

There is one hitch, sometimes public relations companies have relationships with airlines which can mean the airline ticket is complimentary. If this is the case, don't be disappointed, be gracious. Remember, your attitude and manners can help determine whether or not you are invited back on future visits.

Press trip myths

You may be surprised to find that the press trips themselves are actually work. Now, it's true the first night of a group trip – when the destination flies in several writers – is usually the most fun. You arrive at your destination, then meet the rest of your travel companions at a cocktail party or reception. Everyone bonds and has dinner together before retiring to their rooms. The following days are then filled with action-packed itineraries, as you read in Chris Gray Faust's story, which may include museum tours and resort hopping – you may tour as many as three to five resorts, interviewing numerous people, such as chefs, business owners and local experts – whether you care to or not.

And, yes, there is food. Lots of food. Of course, every trip is different. One of my most memorable trips – food wise – was to Shreveport, Louisiana. It was a culinary tour and everyone kept feeding us. Every museum and factory tour wanted us to taste what they had to offer – from coffee and cake to sausage and jambalaya. By the end of the trip I had one pair of pants that fit. I promised that was the last culinary trip I would ever take.

Another myth is that travel writers lead a lively, party life. While the actual travel part can be fun, adventurous and social – watch the travel streams on Twitter and it certainly can appear that way – the actual work can be lonely, demanding and tedious as you sit in your office – or sometimes your hotel room – trying to sew together sentences, meet a word count, and crop and resize photos, and, most importantly, trying to find an editor to buy your work. That can take months or even years.

After your return home, your host will be expecting articles and blog posts about your trip and while online publications are acceptable you do get extra points for the preferred print outlets, like newspapers or magazines, since such exposure is harder to land. However, remember many print publications don't accept work from writers who have been provided with free travel. Keep in mind, if you don't deliver, the invitations will stop. But you must also take into consideration the cost of travel such as checking your luggage, airport parking, and pet sitting. If you have a family you may need to figure out the details of child care and plan what the family will eat when you're out of town.

Press trips are something for the aspiring travel writer to aim for, but you must first establish yourself as a professional before you make it on to these golden lists. Kimberly Button, author and freelance journalist (http://kimbutton.com) can attest to this:

> 'So many people want to get into travel writing to see the world, but those assignments don't come until you've proven yourself. Save money and the expense of travelling on your own dime by discovering your own backyard, pitching little known aspects and topics to magazines of all genres and build up your clips. From there, you'll be able to generate press trips to further reaches of the globe.'

Finally, a warning: sometimes what appears to be an invitation to a press trip is actually a 'pre-invitation' email. What this means is the PR people send out a massive number of 'invitations'. Then, after receiving responses from interested journalists, they choose those writers who can provide the best coverage. This can be rather discouraging when a writer passes on other opportunities because they think they've been accepted on a trip, only to be denied only weeks before the trip.

Dress to impress

Considering that you are on a professional work trip, your attire needs to be appropriate and tasteful. Depending upon the type of trip you're on, the outfits you need to pack should run the gamut from comfortable active wear for adventure trips to nice slacks and shirts for a more conservative itinerary. If you're travelling internationally, prepare for ethnic dress. Ask your planner if you need to bring any special clothing or accessories. For example, in the Middle East headscarfs are common attire for women. You may be required to attend 'get to know you' cocktail parties and last night dinners, so consider packing for an evening or two out.

The unexpected costs of hosted trips

It doesn't take long for first-time travel writers to figure out that sometimes the fee paid for an article assignment doesn't cover the cost of a trip. For example, a few years ago my family was invited to partake in a promotion for an online travel booking company. We were to make plans via the website for the city of our choice and I was to write about the experience. We chose Orlando. We made our reservations, packed our bags and flew to Florida. While parts of the trip were compensated, there were plenty of things we needed to pay for on our own, such as gas, meals and souvenirs. But there was one situation we encountered that we did not plan for and that was unexpected, inclement weather. Rainy weather isn't new to Florida but we happened to visit in 2010, the week it snowed in all 50 states. Not realizing a cold front was moving in until after we landed, we had left our warm winter clothes at home, packing light sweatshirts with plans of layering if it turned chilly. Our one and only day at Disney World was spent running from cover to cover seeking refuge from the all-day downpour. We bought onsite ponchos for the entire family, which helped a little, but by mid-afternoon our clothes were soaked and the children's teeth were chattering. We headed for the gift shop and bought hats and gloves for each of us. Our total expense caused by the weather was over $200 (£175). The lesson: always prepare for extra expenses no matter who is picking up the tab.

ASK WHAT'S INCLUDED

As awkward as it may be, inquiring about what expenses are included can prevent uncomfortable situations or unexpected bills. During another experience my family was hosted at a property and we were told the stay was going to be completely complimentary. However, at the end of our stay we were handed a bill for several hundred dollars for gratuity. It was an expense we hadn't planned for and while we agreed that the stay was well worth it, it would have been better to know we were expected to pay for it. In addition, I never made that money back in article sales.

While I've never encountered this before, I've heard stories of press trip attendees charging things such as food, drinks and massages to their room and expecting the host to cover these expenses. When the bill arrives they fly into a fit of anger. No one should ever expect or assume that anything is free unless the trip host says directly to you that it's okay to charge a meal or drinks to your room.

Expect to receive an itinerary which will depict a dress code for your trip. Often, the weather and conditions of your trip should be listed, too. If not, don't hesitate to enquire. For example, in the weeks before my trip to Québec City, which included a night in the Hôtel de Glace, I received a list of items that I should pack. It was very thoughtful of the people hosting the trip to take the time considering I lived in the Arizona desert at the time and was visiting a very cold winter region. Of course, most times packing for the climate is common sense: if you're going to a tropical setting you know to bring light clothes and a swimsuit and if you're visiting a damp climate pack a raincoat and umbrella.

If you don't receive an email detailing what you should bring, don't hesitate to ask. In addition to the predicted weather and temperatures confirm what type of activities you should be packing for such as hiking, activities (bike riding, horseback riding).

Questions to ask before going on a press trip:

▶ What is the expected weather?

▶ Do I need any special clothing (swimwear, rain or snow gear, layered clothing, ethnic attire)?

▶ What activities will we be expected to partake in?

DON'T BELIEVE EVERYTHING YOU HEAR

PR people do everything they can to ensure the journalists they are hosting receive nothing but the facts. However, that doesn't always happen, especially if you are temporarily put in someone else's care.

Several years ago a group of writers and I were picked up at the Phoenix airport and transferred via shuttle to a northern region of Arizona. The shuttle driver who was not involved with the tour other than being our transportation driver talked the entire journey, telling stories and pointing out interesting landmarks and unique attributes of the dessert. As an Arizona resident, most of the information was familiar, but some of it was new to me and I was rather impressed with this man's knowledge and enthusiasm about the desert. I jotted down notes as he spoke and took photos as the landscape passed us by.

About half way to our destination, the driver began to relay a story that supposedly happened to his cousin. As his narrative started his audience's intrigue was piqued, but as the story's suspense grew I began to recognize the story as a legend I had heard in my childhood. The driver's story was even more embellished than the accounts I had heard but he kept reiterating that the story was true.

The other journalists scribbled as fast as they could as the driver relayed his tale, waving his hands in the air to emphasize the dramatic details. As entertaining as it was to hear him spice up the story with gripping details it didn't mend the fact that the story was untrue. I kept waiting for him to confess it was a legend. But that moment never came. The notes I had jotted down ended up in the trash since, for me, his credibility was ruined.

This is a reminder to always do your research before quoting anyone and always ensure that the stories you tell as a communicator can be verified.

The 'no freebies allowed' rule

Press trips, while one of the most popular travel writing perks, are also controversial. Some of the top-tier and medium-range publications do not accept articles from writers who have accepted any perks or freebies while researching the article. The publishers want to ensure the articles they are publishing are free of any biased opinions that may have been formed though hosted experiences. This is understandable, as it would be unfair to mislead readers. However, writers argue that publications don't pay enough to cover travel expenses. Can you see the quandary? Most publications with these requirements will ask writers if their story derives from a hosted trip; in these cases, respond honestly.

Granted, this isn't the case for all publications. Wade Shepard, editor of www.vagabondjourney.com, says he doesn't have any problem with his writers taking free trips, as long as the writers submit high-quality, engaging work that sparks the reader's curiosity while teaching them something.

Tim Leffel, editor of the award-winning *Perceptive Travel* and author of *Travel Writing 2.0* (2010) has a similar stance:

> As both a writer and editor, my strong opinion is the only publications that have the right to say 'no press trips' are the ones who pay 100 per cent of expenses on top the article fee. Otherwise it's hypocrisy. And what results, especially at the newspapers still surviving, is 'don't ask, don't tell.'

The joy of CVBs, tourism boards and publicists

Not all travel articles are written in the first person. For example, some round-ups and service articles are not based on the author's experience and instead rely on quotes from other sources. This is where Convention and Visitors Bureaus (CVBs) and tourism boards come in. Nearly every CVB and tourism site has a media page that is specifically designed to assist journalists or writers with their fact checking and story details. You can also fill out a form if you would like to request a visit to assist in your story's research. The employees behind these organizations also have fantastic connections and can help you with fact checking and sources.

From time to time editors may ask for professional images and tourism organizations usually have a nice selection of high-quality photos that can accompany your article without cost.

Travel journalist Paul Eisenberg, urges new writers to consider everyone a possible source, but especially be congenial to publicists:

> *A publicist is often trying to sell you on a client or product that you have no interest in, and the most benignly neglectful thing you can do is not to respond to their pitch, and I am certainly guilty of that all the time. The problem is, over time, that the publicist may have something you want the next time around, or may switch agencies, or whatever. And if you're completely unresponsive – or worse, disdainful or nasty, which is something I see new writers do for sport sometimes – you are potentially burning a bridge that would have yielded something really good later on. So I guess my main tip is to try to work some time into your day to interact – not just with publicists, but anyone trying to give you information – even if it's just to say, 'that client or service or destination is not for me right now, but please feel free to keep me posted about other things,' because that simple gesture might, even a year later, yield something that is spot-on for something you want to write about.*

Case study: Press trips – the PR point of view

Kara Rosner (Twitter: @TravelPRpro) is a PR professional based in Miami, Florida.

Based on my conversations with writers looking to break in to the travel arena, press trips are sought after but often elusive, while more experienced and established colleagues get three, four sometimes five invites a day. So, how do you get in on the action? How do you 'qualify' for this all expense paid travel?

Unfortunately, there's no clear-cut answer and what makes sense for one resort or destination to host you might not for another. Similarly criteria from one PR agency might be different than that of another. (We don't make it easy, do we?) However, with that in mind, here are a few factors often considered:

* **Numbers:** Size matters. Sorry, but it's true. The number of people you reach is important. Even if a PR person is (hopefully) savvy enough to understand that reach isn't the only consideration, and there are other factors to look at, it is still one of those considerations. And no, there's not a magic number of how many people you need to reach in order to qualify, because again, there are other factors to consider that can push that number up or back on a sliding scale.

* **Niche:** The good news is that reaching a targeted market also matters. For example, a ski resort that can reach an audience of 5,000 ski enthusiasts through your blog can have equal, if not more of, an impact than a publication that reaches 50,000 people who may or may not care about skiing. So sell yourself to the right resort or destination based on who your outlet caters to, and you'll have a better chance of attending one of their trips.

* **Social influence:** Tweet. Facebook. Twitpic. Instagram. Flckr. YouTube. Be social. Put yourself out there. Your social influence is another important factor when it comes to press trip consideration – both when it comes to real time posting while you're travelling and when promoting your article after the fact. Again, it's a combination of the number of people you have the potential to reach and the quality of those people.

* **Variety:** If you write for a few different smaller outlets – say so. Acknowledge that you may not be writing for a 'big dog', but you're writing for three smaller publications that each reach a different, targeted audience. Bang for the buck. Three for the price of one. The beauty of being a freelance writer. Multiple outlets have value to a resort or destination.

With all that said and done, once you make your way on to a press trip, here are a few tips to help make it a success (and get yourself invited on the next one):

* Do show up on time to all planned activities, meals, departures, etc.
* Don't forget your passport at home and/or miss your flight, ride, etc.
* Do take notes/pictures/ask questions – show that you're paying attention and retaining information.
* Don't wait until a day before the trip to request special arrangements/ activities/interviews needed for your story. Plan ahead.
* Do be sociable – both on Facebook and Twitter and in person with the group.
* Don't go on a trip if you know you can't produce.
* Do send your published blogs posts and articles to the PR rep after the trip. Even better (and much appreciated), send it with the current stats on your publication or site, or number of clicks, or any sort of data you might be able to provide that they might not have access to.
* Don't have 'just one more' glass of wine... six times. (Yes, we have blacklists too.)
* Do enjoy yourself – after all, that will be reflected in your article. If you have a good time, your writing will show that and ultimately it's a win-win for everyone.

How to interview a source

Sources can be the godsend of an informative service article. Finding someone who has knowledge, insight and information on your topic will enhance your non-fiction article, add a personal perspective and oftentimes be the heart and soul of your piece. Freelance travel journalist Paul Eisenberg urges writers to fine tune their reporting skills:

> 'We are all born with the urge to ask questions, but over time, through a lack of interest or curiosity, or laziness, or just being too tired, we suppress the urge. So that means if you're on the phone with a source for a half hour and not getting what you need, do you make-do with what you have, or do you give it five more minutes? Likewise, if you're reading a press release about a product or destination with an eye toward writing up an item, do you make-do with what you're reading, or do you pick up the phone and ask those two or three questions that you know would make the item better?

As a travel writer, there have been times when I've taken that easy way out and cut off the phone interview before getting what I needed. And likewise, there have also been times when I've made-do with the canned material when I didn't have the time or energy to ask those extra questions. And what I can tell you with certainty is that those times when I have stayed on the phone for a few extra minutes, something serendipitous often happens, and the source will give me something good. Or, that extra ten to twenty minutes of following up on the press release to get more answers has yielded good information that I've been able to use. So it's those times when I've pushed myself as a reporter that my travel writing has been more successful. In short, always ask the extra question.'

▶ **Tips for interviewing a source**

▶ Write down name, contact information, title and how the source likes to be referenced (owner, professor, doctor, or author).

▶ Ask for detailed replies by trying to avoid yes or no responses.

▶ Quote the source's exact words. Misinterpreting or misquoting the source is unprofessional as well as misleading and can cause problems including lawsuits.

▶ Find out how people like to be interviewed. Some people prefer to write down their responses while others prefer to talk in person, on the phone or even Skype.

▶ Use a digital voice recorder or your phone to record your conversation. Most importantly, remember to ask the source for permission to record the conversation.

▶ If you do interview via email, feel free to clarify any confusing statements and correct any grammar mistakes. If a word is misspelled and may be confused with other words, check with your contact to clarify exactly what they meant.

▶ Maintain good notes. Include facts such as names, titles, dates, places and events.

Focus points:

Treat press trips as business trips by adopting a professional demeanor.

Look for the unique angle as well as trends while travelling.

Follow through on your promise to produce.

Know what press trips are right for you.

Call on tourism boards when needed, they're there to assist you.

→ Next step

Between your idea and its glorious publication there is a step-by-step process that must be followed: researching, identifying the angle, writing the query, approaching the editor, presenting your idea, selling yourself, receiving an offering, negotiating your pay and producing the article. Chapter 6 is going to help you get there by taking you on this journey step by step.

Pitching Your Idea

In this chapter you will learn:

- ▶ *How to recognize your audience*
- ▶ *How to write a query*
- ▶ *How to connect with editors*
- ▶ *How to handle rejection*
- ▶ *How to write an invoice*

For first-time writers, approaching an editor can be daunting. But as a travel writer you need to put away your insecurities, don your confidence robe and show your dream editors that you are capable of producing outstanding work.

At this point you should have a general idea of print and online opportunities available but there are also some helpful ways to cut down on your publication research time. For example, the *Writer's Market*, aka the writer's bible, comes in two forms – the thick, annual print version that you can purchase online or in book stores and the subscription, online version.

This extensive book is how I found markets when I first started writing. *Writer's Market* provides thousands of print and online international publications, literary agents, book publishers, contests and awards, and helpful articles and interviews with experienced writers. You'll even find a pay-rate chart to reference for freelance assignments. If you choose the online version, you can manage your submissions with various record keeping tools.

Try it now

Like writing on any topic, much of the work of a travel writer is spent finding new markets, querying editors, self-promoting, writing long hours, submitting invoices and organizing the business details. One of the best ways to seek new markets is to see where other travel writers are getting published. Try searching Twitter or Google for travel writers then visit their personal websites for ideas of places to pitch articles. Keep a notebook with possible outlet options.

Know your audience

Before pitching any ideas to an editor, you need to identify your target audience and then find the publication suitable for your idea. You need to consider the following:

- ▶ age
- ▶ life stage – college, parenthood, empty nesters?
- ▶ gender

- race
- sexual preference
- culture
- religion

Remember this

Writing is never about you. It's about the reader.

If you're feeling perplexed about who exactly will be interested in your story, think like a marketer. For example, it's unlikely that most seniors will have any interest in the latest night club opening, and family travellers will probably not find any interest in casino renovations (unless there is a kids' club opening up). Once you know who you are writing for, you will be able to target the proper publications.

If it's apparent that a topic or story angle is ideal for a niche group rather than the masses, then the publication you should be approaching should either market to that certain group or even be a trade magazine.

Try it now

Open a publication you'd like to write for and flip through the pages. You can figure out a publication's audience by looking at the advertising. Is the market for single professionals, empty-nesters, or young, active parents? Fine tune your observation skills by paying attention to the advertisements on TV and taking note of what is being shown at various times of day. Before you know it, you will be a pro at picking out markets and this will help you be a better salesman for your work.

Once you have identified your audience, then it's time to find the publications that fit. 'I suggest that writers really know their markets – know which magazines and websites are open to what kind of writing,' says freelance travel writer Rolf Potts. 'If you aren't passionately familiar with the content and format of a given outlet, odds are you'll never land a story there.'

Anything is possible

Amy Nelson, Features/Travel editor, St. Paul Pioneer Press in Minnesota says, 'It does appear to be more difficult for emerging freelancers (or at least new to me) from when I started as the travel editor four years ago, but I do still read pitches and did just accept a proposal from a local freelancer who will blog for us.'

Nelson's advice for burgeoning travel writers:

> 'Know who you are pitching to, have a specific pitch, be able to provide high-resolution art, make sure the newspaper hasn't covered the location in past six months, disclose if you are attending on a FAM tour or other press junket. Read the publication and offer something they may not have (and may not know they are missing – i.e., trend pieces instead of a destination story, regional travel to nearby locations instead of exotic destinations). Be able to tailor your story to those readers.'

PRODUCING PHOTOS

Vibrant photos are the staple of a good travel piece, especially in a newspaper section. If this is your goal, a good camera is worth the investment. 'With reduced budgets and news space, I think it's much more difficult for new freelancers to get printed and win contracts' says Nelson, 'I also think there's a bigger emphasis on getting good images along with good reporting. I'm not really interested in a remote location if I can't secure art for it. Also, we in the newspaper industry are being pushed to think radically: put digital first. If you can offer digital content along with/instead of your traditional first-person travel destination narrative story, you're at an advantage.' We'll visit this subject in more detail in Chapter 11.

GET CREATIVE

'Don't just pitch to the Travel editor,' suggests Nelson, 'maybe your regional travel story could be used in the Dining section or Sports section if you are focusing on a specific event. Also, don't forget the digital component – photo slideshows, audio, blogs, etc.'

The more details, statistics and facts you include in your pitch, the more polished and professional you will come across.

PRE-TRIP PITCH

There are two ways to pitch a story idea, before the trip or after. Before you pack your bags for your next trip, it's helpful if you can land an assignment before you go. By knowing what you need to produce you will have an insight into what information you need and exactly what angle you are looking for.

WHAT EDITORS NEED

Last week I attended a writers and editors speed dating event. All of the editors attending represented print publications and each had something in common. They were looking for unique angles or insider stories. For example, the golf magazine editor I spoke with explained that his writers need to have insight into the sport in order to find the ideal stories. In other words, it's unlikely the average writer will be able to find the type of story he's looking for, which mainly entails human interest, although it could include a travel angle. Tip: If you're a golfer this could be an ideal outlet for you.

With the other publications many of the editors were excited to hear that I focus on travel because they don't get a lot of travel pitches. The key, they said, is finding that hidden gem-angle.

Try it now

If you have an upcoming trip, take time for some preliminary research. Visit the tourism or convention and visitor's website for unique story ideas and angles. The next time you're at a restaurant or bar talk to the waiter or bartender to get inspiration. When something intrigues you, claim the topic, research more and dig up facts and information then query several editors on your list offering the most unique angle you can find on the subject.

JUST GO FOR IT

Not having any clips may seem like a deterrent, but that didn't stop freelance writer Anna Maria Espsäter (http://annamariaespsater. co.uk) of London. She had a life-long dream of developing a successful freelance writing career but juggling two full-time jobs made her pursuit seem impossible. When the stress became too much to bear she decided to reduce her workload to one job, but within two months her other job ceased and she found herself jobless. 'I had a holiday booked to Cuba at the time and after some deliberation I decided to go despite not having a job waiting for me upon my return,' she recalls. 'The trip was fantastic, truly inspiring and relaxing and I returned to the UK buzzing with ideas and joie de vivre. Shortly after getting back I attended an event in London, where I met a guy launching a new travel magazine and completely on the spur of the moment I asked him if he'd be interested in a feature on Havana.' Despite her lack of experience the editor commissioned her to write a feature for the following issue.

> 'When the feature came out I could hardly believe my own eyes, it looked so good – five pages with my text and images, not to mention getting paid as well. That was the boost of confidence I needed and I haven't looked back since. Over the last six years I've worked on roughly 250 features for some of the best-known newspapers and magazines in the UK, as well as over a dozen travel books and I've been able to travel the world in the process. Of course there's been some hard work involved, but it's mostly been a case of daring to talk to people and being open to opportunities. If you really want something, I'd say just ask for it and see what happens.'

Writers' guidelines

Every publication has requirements for their editorial process. Back in the 'olden days' writers had to request guidelines by writing to the publication via snail mail. A self-addressed stamped envelope needed to be included to guarantee a response. The response could easily take weeks.

Today, all it takes is a visit to the publication's website. Sometimes there is a direct link to the guidelines on the main page and other times you will find the link under 'contact us' or under 'questions and answers'. You may also try punching 'writers' guidelines' or 'editorial submissions' into the site's toolbar, or entering the phrase and the publication's name into Google.

What you'll find listed under 'writers' guidelines' are answers to all of your questions and other important information. Expect to find:

- the assigning editor's name and email address, or a generic editor email

- whether they prefer a pitch or the finished article

- what the lead time is: the time between article acceptance to published

- themes and topics that will be considered

- sections that are available for writers to pitch: features, front of book, back of book and word count of each

- rates of pay for articles and photography

- rights purchased

Query basics

The next step is to work your magic by producing a tantalizing query letter, which is also called a pitch. This letter is a writer's best friend because it saves us the time and hassle of writing a story that may or may not sell. It gives the editor the opportunity to ask for an angle, side bars (brief articles that accompany an article) and word count. And most of all it allows us access to editors.

While it may seem practical that an editor would want to pick a story and have you run with it, the fact is, editors are too busy assigning their staff stories and proofing freelance stories. That's why the query letter is important.

How you present your idea is up to you. It's unlikely every query will follow the same structure every time, but every pitch will follow some general guidelines. Some query letters start off with a clever saying to catch the editor's experience. In others, the writer asks an intriguing question or begins with some interesting rhetoric.

The traditional query gets to the point in only a couple of paragraphs. You address the editor by name, pitch your fabulous idea, explain why you're the person to write it by listing your experience, thank the editor for their time and politely close.

A query:

▶ has a formal salutation and professional introduction

▶ is addressed to the appropriate editor

▶ is a punchy summary of your idea(s)

▶ is a quick sell of your experience

▶ piques interest by offering interesting first-hand experience, solving a problem, answering a question, or revealing new information (such as openings, upcoming events, news or a new spin on an old topic)

▶ is absent of spelling and grammar errors

▶ is timely

▶ is publication appropriate

▶ offers to provide clips of previous work

▶ is friendly

▶ is factual

▶ is not too personal (don't mention non-relevant information such as your pets, kids or significant other)

A query should not:

▶ include your full biography

▶ include the entire article (unless a publication requests it)

▶ demand publication or an assignment

▶ cover old news

▶ discuss payment

▶ ask the editor to visit your website

▶ reveal if the idea has been rejected before

- mention copyright information (screams newbie)
- discuss your lack of experience
- give the editor a deadline to respond (but you may follow up)

Remember this

Consider the query a test. An editor can tell by a writer's query letter whether the sender has any future at the publication.

KNOW THE PUBLICATION

Before you approach an editor ensure you are familiar with the publication by studying recent copies of the issue. When you send your query you will want to have an idea of where your piece will fit in. Below are some of the types of articles in a magazine.

- **FOB (front of book) or BOB (back of book).** Short, sweet, and punchy are normally what describes FOBs. These articles are very short snippets of information, news, openings and events. Such pieces are also the best way to break into a publication since these are like tester pieces given to new writers to see if they can follow through.

Try it now

Research new openings or news in your area. Perhaps your local zoo is expecting the birth of polar bears, a new ice bar is opening up in the city this weekend or a new river cruise is launching daily tours. Write a brief and exciting copy answering the questions – What makes it hot? Why now? Who will care?

If you have more than one idea, FOB or BOB are acceptable sections to pitch more than one idea.

After you have your newsworthy blurb(s), draft a query letter using the information from Chapter 6.

- **Features:** These are the pretty spreads found in the Sunday newspaper's travel section and multi-page features in travel and leisure magazines. They are also where the money is because of their length and the amount of research that goes into them. These beautifully articulated pieces describe colourful scenery, regional fare, aromatic flora and exhilarating activities found in the featured destination. The photography and lengthy descriptions uncover what makes the place a worthy place to visit. Destination feature articles are the reason travel writing often tops dream job lists.

▶ **Profiles:** Profile articles normally feature a person, especially celebrities or other interesting personalities. Such pieces can be written in third-person or in a question-and-answer format. An easy angle to use here is to pitch a story of an up-and-coming chef from your local town.

▶ **Human interest:** These articles might be centred on someone with an interesting story, but they can also be about a town, group, family or organization. These stories are often 'feel good', and can be easily found in your own backyard. At the other extreme, human interest stories can be exposés, revealing some sort of secret. This is where your sleuthing skills will come in. Airlines, hotels, restaurants, cruise ships and even the travel writing profession itself (famous authors writing under pennames) have been victims of this type of writing, which is more journalistic in style with the emphasis on facts and sources.

▶ **Sidebar:** During a visit to a major destination it's very possible that you will take a day trip. For example, my family took a week-long holiday at Flathead Lake Lodge, an all-inclusive Montana ranch. But one day we took a trek to see Glacier National Park and found a number of charming pie and gift shops as well as breathtaking scenery along the way. Such a getaway is the perfect opportunity to find sidebar ideas. These might include facts about wildlife in the area, fun places to eat or scenic stops.

▶ **Service articles:** Also called practical advice or travel tips, these informative pieces reveal sensible information that pertains to travel. Many such articles start with 'How to...'

▶ **Round-up:** Rather than a pen full of sheep, round-ups feature lists such as top tens, 'the best of ...', or other similarly titled articles. Examples are 'The eight whitest Florida beaches', 'The top ten bistros in Paris' or 'The best family-friendly safaris'.

- **Essays:** The essay is a first-person account. These stories are pre-written and sent finished to editors. Often such stories are published on the last page of a magazine but you can also submit these to anthologies. They are often humorous or inspirational.

- **Travel literature:** Stories telling of self-discovery, unfamiliar cultures and exotic lands are revelations stemming from personal experience. Written with literary value, they are the goal of travel literature. After reading these first-person works the reader is left pondering the meaning of the writing or is inspired enough to pack their bags to chase a similar experience. Think Hemingway and John Steinbeck.

SURF THE PUBLICATION'S WEBSITE

Nowadays many articles that appear in print end up posted on the publication's website. Before pitching a story idea do a search on the site to see if your topic has been covered. If the story was covered in the last couple of years, don't bother. But if the article was done many years ago, develop a new angle and pitch it to the editor. Don't hesitate to mention that you saw the old article and explain why yours is new and improved.

Editor Amy Nelson of the Pioneer Press says it's obvious when writers didn't do their homework when they pitch stories of a location that the paper featured in the past six months.

If your editor is new to the publication they will likely do a search to see if the topic has been covered in recent years, so you might as well jump ahead of the game. It shows you're doing your research and are creative in that you can think of new angles to old topics.

Case study: pitching tricks

Charyn Pfeuffer is a freelance journalist, specializing in food, travel and lifestyle topics. Her work has appeared in more than 100 media outlets. From editor and copywriter to marketing and social media consultant, Pfeuffer's 14-year career in publishing and media has involved her in all aspects of telling the perfect story. She can be found on Twitter at @charynpfeuffer. She shares her pitching tricks with us:

'When pitching, I tend to stick to the basics – who, what, when, where and why. I don't get too caught up in giving editors some flashy song and dance – my pitches tend to boil down to, 'here's why my idea kicks ass, here's why it's a timely fit for your publication, and here's why I'm the perfect woman to write the piece'. If there are expert sources I can weave into a piece, I make sure to make those people and connections known. My pitches tend to include a suggested title, sub-headline and maybe a two or three short paragraph pitch. If it's a brand new-to-me publication, I'll include my resume and links to a few current writing clips. I know what my online attention span is like receiving 100+ pitches each week, so I'm mindful to make sure that my words are worth reading. Fourteen years into freelancing full-time, I find it's easiest to sit down once a week (I set a few hours aside on Monday) to pitch story ideas. If I skip a week, it's no big deal. I keep a notebook in my purse and index cards in my car, bathroom and next to my bed, where I jot down story ideas. I also keep a running document on my computer with headings for all my current publications, as well as a sundry list of ideas for 'wish list' publications and stories 'to be placed'. Every story has a home – it's just a case of finding it.'

THE ANGLE

Before we delve into the art of the query letter and how to make contact with an editor, there is something that many novice travel writers misunderstand about travel writing: a destination is *not* a story. Telling an editor that you're going to Iceland and asking if they want a story on it will not land you an assignment. It may even earn you the amateur badge and an eye roll. Editor Chris Anderson of the Huffington Post explains:

'Don't automatically think that what you're doing is original. One of the biggest difficulties in travel writing is making what's already been discovered seem new and interesting. For example you could go to Shanghai and visit The Bund, the French Concession, Jing An Temple, the Pearl Tower and take a calligraphy class and have a smashing time, get lots of great photos, and be happy with your experience. All of those locations might be new to you, but they've all been written about to death, and if you're planning to pitch an editor a story, you better bring something more interesting to the table than the typical experience.'

How do you know what's been written about? Anderson goes on:

> *'Look in your guidebooks, read local city blogs and see what's already been done to death then plan your trip around finding the experiences and people not written about a million times. You can always start with the tried and true and branch out, but never make the mistake that people want to read about your visit to the Eiffel Tower. They don't.'*

Case study: The angle

Alaska magazine's 'writers' guidelines' explains 'the angle' perfectly:

> Whether it's a history piece on Aleut baskets or an adventure tale about hiking in the Brooks Range, it should always have an 'only in Alaska' aspect. A story on a mall in Alaska, for example, won't work for us; every state has malls. If you've got a story about a Juneau mall run by someone who's also a bush pilot and part-time trapper, maybe we'd be interested. If you've got a story about a village store in Chevak where everyone from the surrounding Bush meets to swap gear and tall tales – let's talk. The point is Alaska stories have to be vivid, focused and unique. Alaska is like nowhere else – we need our stories to be the same way.

Try it now

Find that unique angle that will make an editor jump at your idea:

- **Food:** Have you tried a unique food or an interesting cocktail concoction while travelling? What are the food or drink's roots? Is it a new trend or a classic cultural staple?
- **People**: Think of someone you've met on your travels or even someone in your family or friendship ring who has an interesting story that's related to travel.
- **Event**: Is there a big anniversary or interesting festival on the horizon that could make for an enticing story?

After you have chosen your topic, describe your idea and what makes it special. Include dates, relevant sources (if people-focused), facts and any other dazzling details.

APPROACH PROFESSIONALLY

When addressing a first-time editor it's protocol to use a Ms. or Mr. and the editor's last name. Once you've established a relationship then you can move on to first name basis. Addressing an editor cordially ensures that you are presenting yourself as a professional. Remember, you never get a second chance to make a first impression and that is certainly true when it comes to editors.

Remember this

If you have a personal connection to the editor, mention it immediately. Sometimes editors don't get past the first sentence or two.

To make a good first impression:
* remember your manners
* check and recheck for typos
* ensure the correct spelling of the editor's name
* check facts
* have patience; every editor's inbox is overflowing – a follow-up after a week or two is acceptable; the next day is not.

THE HOOK

The hook is exactly what it sounds like. The subject should hook the editor into wanting to read more. Identify what makes your story fascinating, then create a statement that proves it. Influence the editor to say, 'Wow! I must have this story in my publication'. Sometimes an editor will ask for a Hed and Dek with your pitch. Hed or head is short for headline or title and dek or deck means subtitle or article summary. Including these two details in your query letter will help editors visualize your article in their publication.

STICK WITH ONE TOPIC

When you're first starting, it's best to pitch one idea at a time. Trying to sell too many topics can be overwhelming and appear scattered. Once you've worked with an editor a few times it's acceptable to offer a list of ideas. By then you will have established a rapport with the editor. However, don't hesitate to suggest that you have other ideas at the closing of your email.

SELL YOURSELF

Producing a successful query shows you know how to write professionally and can offer valuable ideas. But you need to be a salesman not just for your proposed article but yourself.

Show off your experience by including any relevant information such as your previously published work, your website and/or blog, relevant education, current or past careers, anything else that shows your credibility.

MAKE A CONNECTION

If you have friends in common, belong to the same writing organization or have any other connection be sure to mention it immediately. If only for the reason the editor will be more likely to remember you later on. Editors have full inboxes all day long and you want yours to stand out as much as possible while being as professional as possible.

Case study: approaching editors

Don George is well-known in the travel writing realm. Twenty years ago he co-founded of The Book Passage Travel Writers and Photographers Conference in San Francisco, which has helped launch many writers' and photographers' careers. He is also editor at large and book review columnist for *National Geographic Traveler*, special features editor and blogger for Gadling.com, and editor of GeoEx's online magazine, *Recce: Literary Journeys for the Discerning Traveler*. When asked what advice he has for new travel writers he says:

'I've tried to condense everything I've learned about travel writing and publishing into my book, The Lonely Planet Guide to Travel Writing *(Lonely Planet, 2nd Edition, 2009). I guess my first piece of advice would be this shamelessly self-serving tip: Buy my book! Beyond that, I'd say:*

Know your subject. Write about something that impassions you. Become an expert on it. Infuse your writing with your passion and your expertise.

Know your story. Every piece you write has to have a point: by the time you finish your story, you should know what point you're trying to convey to a reader. Re-read your story and delete anything that doesn't contribute to making that point.

Know your market. Are you writing for your own blog, the local Sunday travel section, a national magazine, or an annual anthology of 'Travelers' Tales'? Tailor your piece to the publication/outlet you're targeting. Know that outlet so well that you basically inhabit the head of the editor/ producer and understand, from their perspective, how it is put together.

Pay attention to illuminating details. Take copious notes on the road. Put it all together back home (unless you're permanently on the road, in which case you're always at home).

Silence the voice in your head that asks, 'Who cares?' You care! And if you pour your care into a piece, readers will care, too.

Attend workshops and conferences and other events where you can network with other travel writers. Network, learn, share. Repeat.

Don't rely on travel writing as your sole source of income.

Don't give up!

An actual query

Below are sections of a real query that landed me a feature in an inflight magazine, minus a few personal details.

(Professional Intro) Dear Mr./Ms. [Editor's surname],

(Hook) Arizona's Historic Route 66 is booming with such character and intrigue that kids actually remove their iPod earphones and stop text messaging friends back home as families successfully recapture the thrill of a classic summer vacation adventure. While much of the original two-lane highway between Chicago and Los Angeles has been superseded by the Interstate Highway System, Arizona boasts the longest stretch of the original Route 66 – 159 miles worth – still in use. Some of the fantastic opportunities along Arizona's 66 are...

▶ *(Why you)* I am a freelance travel writer and an eight-year resident of Arizona and have explored Route 66 multiple times.

▶ *(Proof you can write)* I have been published in ... Some examples of my work are attached.

(Cordial closure) Thank you for your consideration. I look forward to hearing from you.

Sincerely,

Your Next Best Writer [your name]

The editor responded the same morning that I sent the query. The feature article was published two months later.

Remember this

Just the facts ma'am. Unless your commissioned article is supposed to be written in first person, there is no room for speculation. Writers are expected to produce the facts and be able to back them up with proof immediately. Enhance your query letter by including facts, figures, statistics, quotes or personal anecdotes or those of your sources.

Read 'Letters to the editor' columns in newspapers or a corrections section in a magazine and you will see mistakes do happen from time to time. Don't let silly oversights hinder your career.

Timing is everything

The length of time between your travels and pay cheque can be weeks, months or even years. Unless you have a working relationship with an editor and are able to snag an assignment before your trip, the more common experience pans out in this order: travel, query, article acceptance, publication, then pay cheque. Many publications have an editorial calendar that is planned out months or even a year in advance.

If you're thinking your article will make for a great feature next month, it's likely it is already too late, sometimes even for online work.

For example, you may attend Carnival of Venice and blog about your experience immediately. However, paying publications won't have any interest in your experience after the event is over. Your goal then should be to work on a query to present to editors later in the year when they're thinking about that timeframe for next year's issues.

When I'm in querying mode, usually with one or two great ideas, I challenge myself to sell the idea. It goes like this:

▶ name the challenge

▶ set a date for queries to be sent

▶ list publications to approach

▶ set a date for acceptance

▶ go for it!

Try it now: Self-challenge

To be a successful travel writer, setting self-deadlines and schedules are important. Since we don't have a boss looming over our shoulder we need to plan out our objectives. The best way to do this, like reaching any goal, is to set long-term, short-term and immediate goals. I like to look a year ahead then break down my goals by months, weeks and days. If you fall behind, simply push back your goals to the next day, week or month. That's what is so great about being your own boss, you can set your own timeline.

Now it's your turn to set goals. Look ahead nine months. What season will it be? If you're reading this in January you'll be looking at the end of summer, beginning of autumn (depending upon where you are in the world). Some topic ideas could be the best autumn festivals, fitting in a last-minute holiday before school starts or why this time of year is one of the best travel periods (fares drop, crowds vanish).

Speaking of timing

The timing of your query to an editor can make the difference between whether your pitch is accepted, ignored or even seen. I've tried pitching every day of the week and, in my experience, I have found mid-week emails receive the most editor responses.

Another query tactic is being able to check in on social media to see if an editor is in the office, out of town, sick or even bored. I recall an editor posting on Twitter, 'My inbox currently has zero incoming emails.' Talk about a perfect time to approach that editor. On the other hand, I've also seen editors announce they're heading to the hospital for surgery or on a two-week honeymoon. Obviously, work emails will not be a priority in those situations. I'm not suggesting you stalk anyone, but it doesn't hurt to visit an editor's public page before clicking send. See more on the topic of editors and social media later.

After you click send...

Waiting can be tedious. Resist the urge to check your email every five minutes for an acceptance letter. An editor's response can take anything from two minutes to two months (or longer). Or never. If you don't hear anything after a week or two, follow up to ensure they received your email. But keep the following Do's and Don'ts in mind.

▶ **Do**
▶ pitch other publications the same idea
▶ write other queries and send them to other publications
▶ brainstorm other story ideas
▶ have a back-up idea to pitch if an editor rejects your first idea

- know your pay requirements
- check your email daily
- keep a thick skin – you must be able to handle rejection to survive in writing
- have determination – you can do this
- try, try again

- **Don't**
- have any expectations
- follow up immediately
- check your email every five minutes
- get discouraged if your pitch gets ignored
- email again to update or change what you said
- rant about editors on social media
- give up

How to connect with editors

Making contact with editors used to seem impossible with snail mail and phone as the only correspondence options. But email and social media have changed that, making editors much more accessible.

A publication's social media sites are a good place to start. Alternatively you can attend writing or publishing-themed conferences and events, or send off an email of introduction to the publication. Always make the most of your network for introductions.

 Try this

The next time you're on Twitter, start a list dedicated to editors. Following editors will offer an insight into their world, and give you the idea of what they're looking for. Editors open to connecting with writers can open an opportunity for you to get on their radar and build a relationship.

CLIPS VS SAMPLES

There's a very good chance editors will ask to see your work before they commission you to write an article or story. There are two ways they go about doing this: one is asking for clips or tear sheets of your published works; the other is a sample.

Sometimes a published clip doesn't represent your actual writing since it has been extensively edited. That's why some editors ask to see samples of your other work. If they are asking for a sample, be prepared to hand over an unedited piece of work. Occasionally writers will have published pieces that have been minimally edited.

In my experience it isn't always best to attach clips in your query letter email because some editors block unknown senders with attachments. To get around this you may send links to your online work or simply offer to send clips of your published work.

You may mention your portfolio website but do not request the editor visit your website – clicking through websites can be time-consuming and irritating. And always include your website link in your signature whether you mention it or not. The editor may click through on his or her own.

ANTHOLOGIES

When first beginning, every writer struggles with the clip quandary. This baffling perplexity can be compared to the long-asked chicken or egg conundrum (even though scientists have recently solved that one).

Editors expect writers to produce samples of previously published work. But how can you have clips if you've never been published?

During my early writing years I, too, struggled with this predicament, but I found an answer: anthologies.

Anthologies are a collection of stories written by various authors. You may have heard of the *Chicken Soup for the Soul* books (Chicken Soup for the Soul Publishing), an anthology series similar to those by Travelers' Tales publishers. There are numerous benefits to contributing to an anthology. You will be paid a flat rate and will probably receive a biography within the book for self-promotion. You may even receive some marketing tools like bookmarks and t-shirts to assist in promoting the book, and be invited to partake in book signings (but beware that you will probably not make any money from such an event if you do). The most important thing though, is you will be published in print which means you will have nice clips to provide future editors. After writing many stories and submitting to a variety of anthologies I ended up with ten books on my bookshelf that hold my stories and proof that I could get published.

But I didn't stop with books. Similar first-person stories were published in the *Christian Science Monitor* (one story was syndicated and was picked up by nine papers across the United States) and many other print and online publications.

BLOGGER'S OPPORTUNITY
There is a good chance many of you own a blog, but have yet to write for another publication for pay. If you are a blogger with a special niche then you have the wonderful opportunity to use that to your advantage. Pitch yourself as a blogger with a brand. Many bloggers have successfully introduced themselves as experts in their topic and end up with regular paying gigs. This topic will be covered more in-depth in Chapter 9.

The positive reply

When you receive an assignment from an editor it's time to talk business. This is usually done by email but can also be done over the phone. Keep a pen and paper handy if you chat over the phone. Your correspondence or conversation should include:

- the subject and type of article (first, second, third person)
- word count
- deadline
- compensation
- kill fee (see below)
- artwork details (do you need to supply? if so, what type, photo size, etc.)

HOW TO NEGOTIATE

Money – it's what makes the world go round. If you're going to be contributing to a publication you deserved to get paid. If the publication is earning money from advertising, you should receive some kind of compensation.

Once in a while an editor will ask what your rates are. If you're greedy and ask for sky-high rates you will probably lose the opportunity. What I've found to work best is to seek out other writers who have contributed to the publication and ask them what their starting pay was. Some publications do increase their rates after a writer has proven their skills.

Other times the editor comes back with a flat rate or per-word amount. You can certainly request more money and, yes, negotiating can be awkward and not always successful. But it never hurts to ask if there is room in the budget for a little more money. You especially have leverage if the editor comes to you with a very short deadline or a topic that takes a lot of research or art work.

When negotiating, don't just ask for money, also request and verify details such as:

▶ a contract

▶ byline (Author credit. Example: By Beth Blair)

▶ two–three-sentence biography

▶ photo

▶ links to your website, and your blog, Twitter, LinkedIn, Facebook, Pinterest...

▶ the best rights possible (see below)

Before you say yes, ask yourself: Can I write the article and meet the deadline? If the answer is yes, sign and return the contract and any necessary tax forms and start writing.

Remember this

Stay true to your values. You don't have to accept every assignment that comes your way. If it's not something you're excited about or if it's a publication you will be embarrassed to be associated with it is okay to say no. Have standards.

Don't write for free. Make sure you benefit in some manner. For example, Huffington Post doesn't pay, but contributors argue that it offers top-notch exposure along with links to their websites and social media pages.

RESELLING AND RIGHTS

It's unlikely you will be able to resell your articles to several online publications but print is a different story. It's possible to sell and resell the same story over and over and over. Some writers boast selling the same story to dozens of publications. This is especially possible if you're selling to regional publications.

You can also re-angle your story and sell a similar story to other publications. The article rights you may come across are:

▶ **One-time rights:** Grants the publication the rights to use your article one time.

▶ **Regional rights:** Grants the publication the benefit of being the only publication within the region to publish your story.

▶ **All rights:** You may not resell that story to anyone anywhere. The publication may sell or republish the story in other outlets with or without a profit to you.

▶ **Book rights:** Some publications such as newspapers may buy all rights but allow you to republish the story in your personal book.

▶ **Online rights:** The publication owns online rights.

It's also possible to write different stories on the same topic, the key is to devise a variety of angles for each piece. For example, a trip to a new restaurant can result in an article about the up-and-coming chef while another article may cover the unique drinks menu.

KILL FEE

This term sounds rather daunting, doesn't it? Fortunately, for us writers it's a good thing. A kill fee means that we still get paid if something happens and our work isn't accepted or doesn't make it to publication.

Kill fee rates can vary from 25 to 100 per cent. This has only happened to me a couple of times. I recall one situation where I pitched a story to a regional newspaper insert. The 300 word piece was accepted for $1/word, but by the time the piece was supposed to run, the print space had been reduced and there was no longer room for my article. The decision was nothing personal and the editor made it clear that the piece was being saved for possible inclusion at a later date. However, I knew that since the article was timely, the article's foundation was about a local festival, it didn't make sense for the story to run unless it was going to be published the following year. As far as I know, the piece never ran. But I did get a 100 per cent kill fee. Yes, I was disappointed not to have the clip to add to my resume, but at least my time wasn't wasted and I received a nice cheque to deposit.

Remember this

When signing a freelance contract with a print publication, always inquire about a kill fee.

INVOICES

Some publications send an invoice template, but more often than not, the writer is expected to submit their own invoice. There is no precise way to do this, but there is some information every invoice should include: your name, address, email, invoice number, publication name, article title, word count and – most importantly – amount due. If you are writing multiple articles for the publication it's often okay to submit them together, although if the pieces will run in different publications, even though the magazines or newspapers may be under the same publishing company, you may need to submit separate invoices to correspond with the month the work was completed.

▶ **Invoice sample**

Invoice 001 (include a number for reference)

Your Name

Address

Phone number

To: Publication Name

Attn: Editor Name

From: Your Name

Social Security Number:

Date: month/day/year

Article Title (word count) Amount Due: $250/£160

Handling rejection

Rejection hurts – if you let it. When I was first getting started as a writer I kept a green folder filled with my rejections. I still have that folder. Some responses were kind and gave me hope and others were downright wacky. That folder holds a variety of correspondence from editors ranging from generic forms to personalized letters explaining that there is always a work in progress on the same subject. On the humorous side, some were addressed to the wrong person while others were riddled with typos.

That folder kept me motivated, because I knew that the more 'no's' I received, the closer I was getting to an official assignment. I knew that one day I would look at the folder and be proud of the efforts I made.

As time passed the 'yes' emails began to arrive. Today, I have a nice selection of travel clips from magazines, newspapers, books and websites. And soon you will, too.

Freelance travel writer and author Rolf Potts has advice on handling rejection:

> '*A travel writing career is something that develops over many years. Grow a thick skin and get used to having your stories rejected or ignored. Remember that editors are extremely busy people, and don't take their indifference as a personal insult. Once you establish a relationship with an editor, don't let it slide. Be friendly, show your competence, work hard and don't take things for granted.*'

Remember this

When dealing with rejection, don't take it personally. There is only so much space in print publications and frequently the topic you wish to cover has already been done in recent years. Simply try again.

A TWIST ON 'NO THANK YOU'

When you first receive a rejection you may have a number of emotional responses. Everyone is different. Stop. Take a deep breath and consider this as an opportunity. This is your chance to keep the conversation going. Unless the email was very clear that the publication is not hiring freelance writers or states that *you* are not a right fit or need more published clips, respond with a thank you then offer new pitch or idea. Like this:

> *Dear Ms. Smith,*
>
> *Thank you for the quick response. Since my last idea wasn't quite what you're looking for I have another idea...*

Then continue with your story idea and don't forget to mention your specialty in the topic or offer to produce artwork if you can. Make the offer enticing. Editors like to have reliable writers who are always producing good ideas. Show that you are one of them.

Regardless of what the response is, never get defensive or nasty. Curt responses will ruin any chance you have for writing for that publication.

Other ways to get in the door

There are many ways to land an assignment. 'The blind pitch', as we just discussed isn't the only way to land an assignment. The following are other ways to get that first foot in the door:

▶ **Write the article.** Some publications like writers to submit an article without an assignment. This is called submitting 'on spec' (on speculation). In other words, if the editor likes it, they will publish it. If they don't, you can try to sell it elsewhere.

▶ **Letter of Introduction (LOI).** Introducing yourself to an editor can never hurt. This letter, best written as an email, is your chance to impress the editor with your credentials and specialty while letting him or her know you are available for any assignments they are looking to fill. You may also want to add that you are open to last minute assignments and happy to be the 'go-to' person for specific topics. You never know when your topic may arise for an assignment and you may be the person to get it.

▶ **Reference.** If you have friends in high places, or at least have friends who are friends with editors, a referral is a nice way to 'get in' since it is human nature to stick with what's familiar. If you can score a reference, then good for you.

▶ **Reputation.** Sometimes all you need is status. When you produce a strong self-image and allow your name to catch a buzz by what you do or specialize in, the editors will come to you.

▶ **Be a source.** Last year a well-known celebrity magazine approached me for a quote about what a newly engaged Hollywood couple should see or do when they spent time in my city during an upcoming visit. Not only did I get my name and blog's name mentioned in the magazine but the editor offered a finder's fee for any additional fun information revealing the couple's social escapades, such as sporting events they attended or restaurants they dined at during their stay. I was travelling when the couple was in town and, honestly, it's not my style to stalk stars, but the lesson here is that you can make a little extra money offering magazines ideas or tips – especially if you have access to insider information. Finder's fees are never guaranteed, but it never hurts to ask. I've heard of newspapers using this same tactic. Most of all, remember to use good judgement. Keep your dignity and don't disparage or ruin someone's reputation just to earn a few bucks.

Once you get the assignment...

When you land an assignment, celebrate your success... then get to work. Turning an article in on time is essential. Some writers outline their articles while others simply dive in. You will discover what works best for you. Set your writing schedule and stick with it. After you complete your piece, let your work sit for a couple of days then re-read it. Often you will think of a better way to say something and discover typos.

Each writer has his or her own writing routine. Some work in the early morning, others work business hours, while others find their best work is done late at night. Find your peak work hours and keep your writing routine to those periods. Make it a point to figure out what your best writing hours are: if you're drowsy or tired, it will be harder to concentrate and perform well.

DON'T MISS THE DEADLINE

Mark Orwoll of *Travel + Leisure* says of the mighty deadline: 'More important than anything – and this comes from me wearing my editor's hat – get your copy in on time. No lateness, no excuses.'

Beware: if you can't meet a deadline because of an emergency, contact your editor as soon as you know. Most importantly, do it *before* the day of the deadline. Not only is this common courtesy, but doing otherwise will ruin your credibility.

Also, don't try to run and hide. A couple of years ago, an editor used Twitter to catch the attention of a writer who missed an article deadline and wasn't responding to emails. In the meantime, the writer was happily chatting away on Twitter about his latest escapade. He obviously wasn't hurt or sick. The editor continued to tweet the writer until the writer finally responded. Not only can such a situation be embarrassing but it can also destroy your reputation as a writer. The lesson: never miss a deadline.

FOLLOWING GUIDELINES

Whether you're pitching a magazine, newspaper, website or blog there is one thing writers must respect and adhere to and that's the publication's guidelines. Style, format and word count are extremely important. If your submission doesn't fit, you don't get published.

Following directions seems like elementary advice, however ask any editor and they are sure to have stories of writers exceeding word counts and submitting stories different to what was assigned. Word count is one of the most important factors, especially if you're writing for a print publication. There isn't room to flub. I had a writer pitch an idea for my travel blog. I accepted the idea and gave her a 500–700 word count. She submitted a 1500 word piece and wrote in her email to me, 'I know you said 500–700 words, but thought I'd write more since you can't go wrong with more words.'

That's not true. When you're working on your article, writing more is fine, but ultimately you must trim it down to meet the publication's requirements – and in the process you will likely develop a better article. This situation caused more work for both of us because she didn't follow directions.

BENEFITS OF AN EDITOR

I love being professionally edited. Seeing changes and corrections gives me the chance to become a better writer and see my work from a new perspective. However, not all writers feel this way. I've been in many writer gatherings where writers express how disheartened they are because an editor tore their piece to shreds.

Writers have and need editors for a reason:

- ▶ to correct your mistakes
- ▶ to find better ways to 'say it'
- ▶ to teach you to be a better writer
- ▶ to help the piece mould to the publication's voice

Editors are not perfect. I've had writer friends who have had to deal with difficult editors who have changed source quotes, made up false statements and introduced typos and grammar errors. The point is, writers and editors are all human and we all make mistakes. If you find an error in your work, bring it to the editor's attention and move on. Overall, you will discover that the editors you work with are helpful and have savvy editing skills, something that can only make you a more efficient and knowledgeable writer.

Try it now

If you're unsure of your writing skills, join a writing group or enroll in a writing class to brush up on your craft and to help you discover your unique writing voice. Every city has an assortment of writing groups and the group you join doesn't have to be travel themed. In fact, it can be good to have an assortment of writers on different topics for new perspectives. Check out MeetUp.com and search for writing groups in your area.

Plagiarism

No book about writing is complete without a mention of one of the all-time no-nos of writing, and that is plagiarism. Stealing the work of others and claiming it as your own is probably the worst offence in writing. Writers have had their careers ruined due to making this one mistake. If you need to reference someone else's writing, be sure to give them proper credit or quote them directly.

Focus points

Take the time to identify your audience.

Perfect your query before sending it. Never rush this step.

Rejection is part of the travel writing game. Don't let it stop you.

Today, writing is more than words. Show your editor you can offer multimedia options and social media exposure.

Keep a professional reputation by never missing a deadline.

Next step

As you can see, landing an assignment is a step-by-step process. After you get the official 'yes', it's time to put your creative powers to work by addressing the conventions and styles of travel writing.

Conventions and Styles of Writing

In this chapter you will learn:

▶ *Ways to write*

▶ *Tips for proofreading your work*

▶ *How to make transitions in your work*

▶ *The one punctuation mark you should always avoid*

Have you ever read a travel article or book and felt as if you were there, accompanying the author during their expedition? If so, then the writer accomplished his or her mission. Good travel writing includes not only proper use of grammar and punctuation, but takes the reader on a journey that emerges naturally though creative writing and descriptions. Readers desire to see what you saw, feel what you felt and, most importantly, they wish to relate to your experiences or, at the very least, be entertained.

As you navigate bringing your story to life, remember that a travel article weaves many different writing aspects. The angle, details and descriptions must meld with an editor's goals, a publication's market and a reader's interest.

The purpose of the article

Every article serves a purpose. Sometimes it's to be helpful and other times it's for pure enjoyment. As you read magazines, newspapers and websites, make it a habit to identify the type of articles you read by asking does it...

- ▶ offer information?
- ▶ solve a problem?
- ▶ influence?
- ▶ entertain?

Reflective writing

Reflective writing is exactly what it sounds like; the writer reflects on a memory, interaction, scene or event, then brings it to life through his words. When working on a reflective travel piece you can ask yourself questions such as: What did I learn? How did this impact me? What did I see, hear, taste, touch? What did I feel?

The following text is taken from an article called 'Three Great Getaways', which I contributed to *Hybrid Mom* magazine (September 2009). I write reflectively from a first-person account of my stay on Providenciales, in Turks and Caicos Islands.

After a while it was time to venture out and explore. Ocean Club has a fleet of beach cruisers and, since it had been well over a decade since I had ridden a bike, I decided it was time to tap into my long lost childhood passion. I hopped upon the seat and pushed the pedals forward. Leaving all elegance behind, I wobbly made my way off the resort grounds and onto a main island street.

As I rode down the street, I encountered the friendliest drivers. Every car passing gave a nice long honk. I waved back, smiling. That was, until I saw other bike riders on the sidewalk. I decided to do the same, and amazingly the honks stopped.

I coasted past rows of palm trees and darting lizards while enjoying the ocean breeze. I felt a sense of freedom I hadn't felt in some time...

Try it now

Do you have a story you can write about in a few paragraphs? Perhaps it has a hint of humour, as in the passage above, or maybe you have something profound and interesting to share. Write your story, or at least the basis for it. It doesn't have to be a long, drawn-out tale – just the meat and potatoes, if you will. Then, when the right angle comes to you, or if you get an assignment, you already have some text to contribute.

Remember, your initial work, or first draft, doesn't have to be perfect with flawless grammar. Simply get the story on the page. Try to do this straight after a memorable experience so you can recall the details more easily.

Imagine you are there, right now. Bring the sights and sounds to life with your words. What did you see, hear, smell, taste and feel? To reiterate, in travel writing it is imperative a reader feels as if they're being brought to the exact location or situation you're writing about. Use the following to inspire you:

- **Sight:** Descriptions should include vivid landscapes, colours and details. Do the city skyscrapers reflect the blue sky or ominous dark clouds?
- **Sound**: Describe the sounds of the region: the beat of the drums, children laughing, gravel roads, ice crackling beneath your boots, the howl of the wind, the screech of a cat. Focus especially on the unique sounds of the area – e.g. culture, nature and music.

* **Taste:** From saltwater in the air to cold ice cream, divulge the tongue's sensations. Culinary stories should be embossed with flavourful descriptions. Describe your food and drink's taste and texture like the hosts on a food show or as experienced sommeliers do. Reveal what you taste and feel by using terms like smoky, bitter, crunchy, sticky, frothy, sweet, salty, earthy and reveal specific flavours, like garlic, dill, ginger or vanilla.
* **Smell.** Every destination, or even street corner, has its own scent. Do you smell street vendors' food smoking, freshly baked bread from a nearby baker or coffee beans roasting?
* **Feel.** Deliver your reader to your location by describing the weather and temperature: damp mist, humid air, scorching sidewalk or slick ski slope.

Bring your destination to life through the senses. Describe what you saw, heard or felt. Was the setting a city, seaside, country, lake, mountains? Describe the weather and temperature – was it hot and muggy or cool and crisp with a light gust in the air? What was the sun doing – reflecting off a nearby river, is there an Alpen glow that is turning the ski mountain a royal purple? If there were people, describe their attire and customs, such as how they greeted each other – with a bow, kiss or handshake?

Persuasive writing

Persuasive writing happens when your purpose is to influence your readers to act, as in pack their bags and leave today, or to change their thoughts about a certain location. While persuasive writing is often associated with politics and causes, it can be used in travel writing. The most common use is after recovery from a natural or human disaster. For example, a couple of years after New Orleans was on the upswing after the 2005 Hurricane Katrina I was invited to witness the city's successful revival. Through my writing, I was able to convey that the city was on the mend and open to visitors with the same spirit and culture this Deep South city was always known for. On the other hand, you may wish to warn your readers to avoid a certain location due to its high crime or other deterrent.

Choose a location that you have been to or maybe even your own town. Think about the off-season. Perhaps it's extremely hot in the summer or too cold in the winter. Maybe it rains for months on end. Turn the negative thoughts around and point out the positives.

For example, when I lived in the Colorado Rockies the period between winter (meaning the ski mountains close) and summer (when tourism picked up again) was called Mud Season (due to the snow melting). While it's an odd in-between season, the ski resorts were quiet, had lower hotel rates and many of the restaurants offered wild food and drink specials to draw in customers. Such an angle would make a perfect persuasive article about why travellers would want to visit a ski town during Mud Season.

Now it's your turn ... try to write a 400-word piece focusing on the benefits of visiting your identified area during off-season. Answer these questions: What time of year is considered off-season? What does the season look and feel like? What are the benefits of visiting during this time? What does the town offer during this time?

Objective writing

Objective writing is what newspapers are based on. Objective writing presents facts, figures and stories in a non-biased manner. When you're writing a non-first person account it's best to be as objective but honest as possible. For example, Mexico has received a bad reputation over recent years because of drugs and violence in certain regions, but this doesn't mean that Mexico should be avoided as a destination. In fact, I have an upcoming trip to Mexico. Most resorts are secure and safe. You can combine both of these facts in your writing.

Case study: what makes a good travel writer?

After Edie Jarolim moved to Tucson, Arizona, from New York City, she authored three guidebooks: *Frommer's San Antonio & Austin* (2005), *The Complete Idiot's Travel Guide To Mexico's Beach Resorts* (1999) and *Arizona For Dummies* (2007). She has also published hundreds of travel articles in national publications including *Brides*, *National Geographic Traveler*, *Travel + Leisure* and *The Wall Street Journal*.

'I've sat on both sides of the travel writer's desk, first as a guidebook editor at Frommer's and Fodor's in New York and Rough Guides in London, now as a freelancer in Tucson. I wish I'd reversed the order of those positions – I'll get to that – but being an editor drummed one key thing into my head: travel writing is about the writing, not the travel.

There was nothing more cringe-worthy among my editor colleagues than to get an inquiry from an aspiring guidebook writer that said: 'I was wondering if you would be interested in sending me to [fill in desirable destination]. I love to travel.' You may have had mind-shattering adventures in remote, inaccessible places where few tourists have ventured, but unless you can convey your experiences effectively through words, you are a traveller, not a travel writer.

And don't even get me started on the request to be sent to a desirable destination without having proved yourself.

So what makes someone a good travel writer, one that an editor will want to hire and keep using?

- Keen observation, with telling details marshalled towards creating an atmosphere or moving a story forward. Details that don't add up to any singular impression or point about a trip are almost worse than no details at all.
- A strong voice. Your readers might not agree with your assessment of a particular destination or attraction but they'll know you have a core set of beliefs about what you like – or don't – that they can depend on. That doesn't mean you need to be overly critical; it's easy to cross the line from irreverence to snarkiness and negativity. Don't try to show how clever you are at the expense of your audience.
- Correct grammar and spelling and, in the case of guidebooks, adherence to the required format. It's disrespectful to assume editors will clean up your mess because that's their job. Yes, they will do that if they have to, but they will not hire you again. I hate to say it, but there are lots of talented writers. Make it easy for editors to choose you by following the rules.
- Meeting deadlines. See 'Correct grammar and spelling...' above.

All well and good you say, but how do I get my foot in the door in the first place? Here are some things you might consider:

* Apprentice yourself to a published travel writer you admire. I had someone offer to help me update my book *Arizona for Dummies*, out of the blue. She did a terrific research job and, when she said she was headed for London and Rome, I told her to contact my former colleagues at Rough Guides; my enthusiastic recommendation led to lots of work for her. Any writer worth her salt will, at minimum, be flattered and do some mentoring in repayment.

* Start a blog. This is mixed advice, because it's easy to devote all your energies to it and not pitch to paying outlets, but if you get a large enough following, you'll be invited on trips, at minimum. Travel PR folks are getting savvy about the reach that online outlets have. And if you don't have published writing samples yet, it's a great way to showcase your voice and style.

* Pick a niche. Become the go-to person for a particular type of travel or destination you like, whether it be boomer travel, pet travel, China.... That way, editors will look to you for expertise.

As for why I regret having been an editor before I was a freelancer, it's because I would done two things differently had the positions been reversed. I would have told the writers who were good how much I appreciated them, instead of just assuming they knew because I kept hiring them. A little praise goes a long way when you're sitting at your computer, lonely and struggling to find the right words.

And – equally if not more important – I would have done everything I could to make sure they were paid on time.'

Self-editing

Final articles aren't produced in the first draft. Non-writers have a preconceived notion that writers sit down and write flawless stories and that's it. This is not the case. A good writer revisits their articles and stories time and time again. Successful writers are always looking to improve their work, find a better word or enhance their story in some way.

Some authors have been known to put their entire manuscript away for weeks, months and even years in order to re-read it with a fresh eye – assuming there isn't a deadline looming.

The point is, always take a little time to read over your piece before submitting your work. Final editing usually tends to take a nice chunk out of our work of art – that's why it's better to write more with the intention of cutting later and still meeting your word count.

WORD REPETITION

In my early days of writing I asked my father, a writer himself, to read over some of my work. One of his comments was to pay attention to word repetition. He pointed out that I was using some of the same terms over and over when many of the terms could be enhanced or replaced with better words. It was some of the best advice I ever received as a writer. Now, not only do I pay attention to my own natural inclination to repeat words, but I observe this redundant habit in other writers.

Keep a thesaurus handy or bookmarked on your computer. Sometimes the perfect word is just a 'look-up' away.

CLICHÉS

Huffington Post Senior Editor Chris Anderson says of clichés:

> *Some of the biggest mistakes a travel writer makes when starting off are pretty easy to identify from an editor's point of view. Clichés. Hate them. Kill them, avoid them at all costs. Flowery travel writing is out. Clichés are lazy and if I get a pitch loaded with 'hidden gems', 'bustling', 'East meets West' I automatically think, 'This is lazy writing' and move on. If you fashion yourself as a writer, a real writer, then act like one and don't fall into the cliché trap. Unless you're writing to some brochure specification or an advertorial, you need to be able to write with a genuine voice and style without resorting to the same old tired clichés.*

EXCLAIM WITH WORDS, NOT PUNCTUATION

As F. Scott Fitzgerald said, 'Cut out all those exclamation marks. An exclamation mark is like laughing at your own jokes.'

If you're already a writer you know the detriment an exclamation point can do to your writing and chances to land an assignment with an editor. Copy riddled with the infamous '!' screams amateur and unprofessional.

Try it now

Pull out some of your previous work and read over it. Count the number of exclamation points. If you have more than one per work this is an area you need to pay attention to.

KILL YOUR DARLINGS

I'm not sure where I first heard the phrase 'kill your darlings' but it is one of the most significant mantras I've learned since writing. What it means is this: having the courage to move or cut words, sentences and phrases that you adore and are proud of but don't add value to your story or article, thus they need to be banished. This step can be hard to do. After all, that word or phrase may sound strong and impressive and was probably one of your favourite additions to the piece.

Remember this

Here's how I kill my darlings. Actually, I don't kill them. I hold them captive. Instead of pushing the delete button I cut the word, sentence or phrase and add it to a saved notes document where I keep my darlings that didn't make the final cut. This way, if I discover a place to fit them in later on I can easily access them. To tell you truth, I rarely revive the words added to the document, but it's nice to know they're there.

Case study: writing and self-editing

Freelance journalist Amanda Castleman (www.amandacastleman.com) is a former wilderness guide who specializes in travel, adventure, the environment and women's issues. Her writing and photography have appeared in numerous international publications and she has contributed to over 30 books, including *Greece, A Love Story* (Seal Press, 2007) and *Rome in Detail* (Rizzoli, 2003).

Here she analyses her essay *'Calm as the Hurricane's Eye'*, which won a bronze Lowell Thomas for adventure coverage.

> When I hit a compositional roadblock, I deconstruct my latest draft – sort of 'reverse-engineering' an outline. The process helps me parse 'what the heck was I thinking and where is it all heading?'

Often, I step away from the keyboard to jar my brain from its familiar grooves. I grab scraps of paper and jot down one word summarizing each paragraph and another its mood. This helps me spot repetitions, examine the narrative arc and ponder how emotions evolve throughout the story. And should I need to restructure, I can easily remix the ideas without full rewrites.

Here's a more extended example of a reverse outline, drawn from a Road and Travel essay about my scuba-certification in Honduras (and consequent blunders). The full story was originally published at www.roadandtravel.com

Emotionally, it follows the impulse to dive down, rather than go slow. The finale concludes that balance is the key (with a dorky bilingual pun even!).

The Roman numerals don't correspond with paragraphs exactly, but with episodes:

I. In medias res (Latin: into the middle of things) lede: humorous anecdote (fishbowl head – a mask full of water on land)

II. Nut graf (the editorial heart of a story): where (Roatan, Honduras), why (traveled 3,000 miles for scuba certification), suspense (will I pass?)

III. Resume dialogue and action from opening scene. Segue on idea of slowness.

IV. Colour about the place: Sensory details. How that mood relates to diving.

V. Anecdote: resumes narrative thread (dive exam), sensory details, dialogue and analysis of the experience. Resolution of earlier tension (mask test accomplished).

VI. Anecdotes, colour and dialogue (the underwater experience)

VII. Anecdote (transitioning out of the sea, resolution of suspense with the announcement I've passed)

VIII. Emotion expressed through action and exposition: connection with the water, the significance of passing the exam (my baby cousin – a tattooed wildcat of a Navy diver – died from cancer seven months ago)

IX. Reverie disturbed (pilot whale sighting)

X. Experience and its context

XI. Reaction (Their appearance, I know, is coincidental, but it still feels like a benediction.)

XII. Anecdote (lateness makes us hustle – the opposite of the 'slow' lesson from early on. I make a bad decision, not for the first time.)

XIII. Outcome (injury)

XIV. More chronological narrative (other hurt divers in the pool, return to opening theme with waiter, the 'slow-haunch' towards the dance, hinting at lessons learned)

XV. Anecdote (fiesta on the cay. The 'punta' [point] dance, celebrating its contradictions)

XVI. Conclusion (metaphors about slow and fast, employing local details. Then a pun about the punta being in between those qualities).

Tips for proofreading your work

Reading and re-reading can't be done enough if you ask me. Here are a few ways to proofread your work:

▶ Two pairs of eyes are always better than one. If this is your first attempt at getting published, rally a friend or family member to proofread your work or query letters before submitting to an editor. Even as you get more experienced you will find it helpful to have someone look over your work. Email your final work to a friend or family member to read over it and catch any mistakes.

▶ Print your article and read it several times. Use a red pen to mark your errors or to make notes.

▶ Read out loud. Hearing your words said aloud will give you perspective on how your work flows as well as the chance to catch mistakes.

▶ Change your article's font on your computer then re-read it. Reading your work in a different style than what that you wrote in will help your eyes catch punctuation and grammar blunders.

Try it now

Because you don't need an assignment to write an essay, develop a first-person story inspired from your past travels. Use your senses, feelings and colourful details to create a first-person account of your experience. Take your time and write the story using everything you have learned from this chapter: enticing introductions, bring the senses to life, use detailed transitions and close with a powerful ending. Wait a few days and reread your piece; edit as needed and invite a friend to be your second pair of eyes. Next, submit your work to a publication that accepts essays.

Focus points

Use all five senses in your writing to bring your destination or experience to life.

Use a tantalizing introduction to draw your reader in.

Use transition words to assist in changes in times and locations.

Finish your work with a solid ending to help the reader feel satisfied.

Get into the habit of proofreading.

Next step

Chapter 8 is going to show you the important elements of a travel article and how to enhance your work so it will keep your editors coming back with more assignments.

Article
Development

In this chapter you will learn:

- ▶ *How to craft an eye-catching beginning*
- ▶ *How to develop a solid middle*
- ▶ *How to finish with a memorable ending*
- ▶ *How to use transitions*

A good article is like a good meal: the beginning, middle and end all contribute to the experience. The title is comparable to the menu, teasing the reader to start the article. The beginning draws the reader in, and the article itself stimulates the reader with information, while the sidebars season the piece with extra flavour. The ending is the dessert that finishes the meal, leaving the reader satisfied and thinking 'Wow, now that was a fantastic read!' This is why it's important to pay attention to every detail of your article.

Outline

While some writers prefer to sit down and start writing straightaway, many writers plan out their article in advance. A good starting point for planning is to break up your outline into four steps:

1 title

2 intro

3 subheadings 1, 2, 3 (depending upon length of piece)

4 ending

You can work on each section in order or dip in and out. Every writer has his or her own habits and techniques. Find what works for you.

Mark Orwoll, of *Travel + Leisure*, explains how to add depth to your article:

> 'The best advice I can give to a would-be travel writer (besides travelling a lot and writing a lot) is to be extra observant. Watch how an Englishman orders a pint at a pub. Listen to the cries of the sellers at a Mexican farmers' market. Learn how to pay your tram fare in Sarajevo or why a cup of coffee with milk and two sugars is called 'a regular' in New York. Details are a travel writer's arsenal. Learn how to interview people; a story without quotes is like flat beer. Become a grammar expert, and increase your vocabulary daily.'

Title

Be forewarned, there is a good chance your article title may get a makeover if it is accepted for publication. Don't take this personally. Editors and publishers know what their readers like and, even though your article title may be cute or clever, it may not fit the publication's remit. However, you can still give it a shot.

Here are some of the titles of my published articles:

- 'Route 66 Road Scholars'
- 'Sit Back and Relax'
- 'Avoid Airport Cash Traps'
- 'Hollywood in the Desert'
- 'Edible Art'
- 'The 5 Best Beaches on the West Coast'
- 'You Say Tomato'

However, despite these titles, many of my online article titles start with *How to* ... or have the word *tips* in, which goes to prove that people love to learn. This is even more imperative as websites continue to keyword their articles and titles. Keep this in mind as you pitch ideas.

Eye-catching beginnings

After the alluring title, the first few lines of a story can make or break the article. That's why 'eye catching' is important. In fact, your article introduction should also be your query introduction. What catches an editor's eye will also please their readership.

Words should be intertwined so that the reader is inspired to read on through to the end. For example, I pulled an *Island Magazine* issue off of my bookshelf and opened the magazine to a random page. The first line of an article written by Matthew Miller is a quote: 'The Secret? Getting your nuts as dry as possible...' I certainly found this first sentence interesting. The word *secret* is rather appealing and I naturally ask the question, what type of nuts is he talking about ... peanuts, walnuts? Readers love stories that reveal information in an engaging fashion and that's certainly is the case for this story about macadamia nuts in Hawaii.

The old saying, 'a picture paints a thousand words' may be true but the opposite is also true for words. The terms you choose can paint a beautiful picture for your readers while also piquing their interest. For example, this was an intro I used for a piece published in the United States insurance company State Farm's magazine *Good Neighbor*.

> *Eight mariachis in black and silver-studded charro attire stood over our table, blowing trumpets and strumming Mexican guitars as my family clapped along. The music ended, and, as if on cue, a waiter delivered warm tortillas, freshly made guacamole and carne asada tacos. It was a delicious end to an adventurous day that began with a visit to a 300-year-old mission...*

Background and facts can be used as a nice foundation for a piece. In a feature for *Arizona Bride* called 'Sit Back and Relax' (Spring/Summer 2009) and featuring regional spas I used this tactic for a reason. The Tucson area is known as a spa mecca and the history dates back over five thousand years. This was the best choice because it explained what made this region special and backed it up with facts.

> *Roughly 5,500 years ago, Native Americans inhabited an area in what is now Tucson's far-east side. Eventually this special spot was named Agua Caliente 'hot water' by the Spanish for the naturally warm spring water filling three large ponds. In 1873, a ranch and health resort was created to tap into the springs' healing power. Since then, southern Arizona has flourished with spas and health resorts dedicated to improving health and well-being. Today, these resort spas provide unsurpassed service, along with numerous fine amenities.*

Stylistic devices, such as alliteration, can be used but it's best to use these sparingly. This passage from an article I wrote called 'Edible Art' for a lifestyle publication named *Oro Valley-Marana Magazine* (August 2008) uses an alliteration method only once; any more than that would be distracting.

> *The Village Bakehouse's glass door swings open and a surge of sweetness fills the air. Behind the counter sits a bevy of freshly baked bread, but it's what is displayed above the bread that catches the eye.* (This line tempts the reader to wonder what's above the bread.)

> *An assortment of cakes in various colours and shapes grace the top wooden shelf. One is pink and white and disguised as two stacked gifts. Next to it sits a balancing, or so it seems, stack of sleek turquoise blue- and white-tipped 'bowls'; each layer is embellished with white diamonds or stripes ...* (These lines answer the question through description.)

Try it now

Using descriptive words in the beginning sets the stage for the reader. Now it's your turn to develop a descriptive introduction. Plan to bring your reader to your location by choosing vivid terminology. Decide on your destination and write one or two sentences depicting the setting while appealing to the senses. If nothing comes to mind, venture out to a local park or café and describe the setting. What do you hear – clinking coffee cups, children laughing, squeaking swings? Or smell – baking croissants, desert rain, sweet lilacs?

The 'meat and potatoes'

The main body of the article should be solid and go into depth about your subject, destination or story. If there is conflict or something curious is occurring then describe the situation and include any interesting details that will enhance your piece. Don't hesitate to ask questions or use quotes, facts, figures and recollections to pique the reader's interest and urge them to continue reading. Most importantly use the five senses to depict your story. Describe sights, sounds, flavours and aromas to draw your reader in but remember to keep your prose moving along to avoid boring your audience.

One way to keep your story flowing and give your reader's eyes a break is to use subheadings to enhance the flow of the article and to prepare the reader for what's next. Make your point valid while adding descriptions to enhance the article and to make the piece an interesting read.

Transitions

Because travel stories usually take readers on a journey, it's important to carefully take note when your article is changing directions since article transitions can be tricky. If not done correctly, the reader can become easily lost or confused. A London piece in *Travel + Leisure* reveals the author using transitions such as, 'After a taxi drops me off...' and 'That evening...' as transitions.

Another piece in the same publication is covering Tokyo's culinary delights. After the introduction the writer transitions with a sentence detailed with the time and a lead that shows adventure is coming: 'At 10 p.m., barely three hours after landing at Narita, the odyssey begins...'

When changing course, use terms like: *consequently, also, as a result, furthermore, nevertheless, soon after, hours later, after departing, the next day.*

Try it now

Keep a note of any transition phrases that you come across. When writing, if you get stuck for transitions pull this list out to jog some ideas as you write. For example:

* As the sun was setting...
* After we took our last sip of coffee...
* When the steaming Pho arrived...
* Following the dance...
* Two hours later...
* Once the bus stopped...

Mastering the ending

Writers often feel an article writes itself. The words magically seem to appear on the page without much effort then toward the end, the words come to a screeching halt. If you don't have a smooth finish, the article will be inconclusive and this leaves the reader hanging and most likely confused.

The same thing can happen with the article introduction. Believe it or not, the beginning and ending have a lot in common. Why? The tactics used to present a successful opening and close are often similar.

Below are several options for wrapping up your piece.

▶ **Quotations**: Nothing ices an article like a solid quotation at the beginning or the end. It works like an exclamation point without using the actual pronounced punctuation.

▶ **Loop:** A loop, also called circular, means the writer refers back to the intro at the close. Here is an example from an article I wrote called 'Professional Travellers' (*Toastmasters Magazine*, 2012). The premise of the piece was how travellers use their speaking skills while on the road.

> *Thirteen years ago, when I was a first-year flight attendant, my airline crew had a multi-day layover at an all-inclusive resort in the Dominican Republic. On our first evening, as we enjoyed the tropical setting, we met a group of resort employees. We discussed the recent hurricane that ripped across the island, and I asked one of the young men if he was a local. He looked at me horrified and hurt, as did his cohorts. His friend defensively asked me, 'Why did you ask my friend if he is crazy?'*

> *After a moment, I realized that the word 'local' had been confused with the Spanish word loco, meaning crazy or insane. What ended in a good laugh was also a lesson for me: Good, non-offending communication is priceless.*

▶ The article continued with examples of why good communication skills are important when travelling and used quotes from travellers about their experiences. The ending summed up the article's premise and 'looped back' to the introduction by referencing the word loco:

> *To ensure positive and memorable travel experiences, don't leave your Toastmasters skills at home. They can come in handy when you end up appearing a little* loco.

▶ After making my point, the article continued and then when it was time to tie up the piece I was able to use the word loco again for a 'complete package' ending.

> *Take note: As you many have noticed, many of the writing examples used merged the English language with terms from other languages: Native American, Hawaiian and Mexican. By using this practice you gently bring the reader to the ethnic side of the destination's culture without bombarding them with too much information.*

▶ **Humour:** Offering your reader a little chuckle is always a fun way to end an article if it's done tastefully and is relevant to the piece.

▶ **Summarize:** This option can come off as a little boring, but it works in a pinch. Simply sum up the article's main points for reinforcement.

▶ **Anecdote:** A personal thought that offers a thought-provoking ending. In 'The Salsa Trail', a first-person narrative I contributed to *Desert Leaf* (September 2008), another Tucson publication, I relayed the story of exploring the Salsa Trail with my husband. The Salsa Trail is a culinary trail in Southeastern Arizona featuring several restaurants and their unique salsas. I drew on our personal experiences and reactions to the different concoctions and quotes from restaurant workers. I end with our last moments on the trail as well as a personal anecdote:

> *The next morning we stopped into El Coronado Restaurant for breakfast and bought a container of its secret-recipe salsa. After scouting out the remaining restaurants in the area we headed home with our eight ounces of fresh salsa. A couple days later, however,*

when we opened our container of salsa to enjoy with corn tortilla chips we discovered the flavour had changed; it didn't taste nearly as fresh. We should have known. Some things are just meant to be experienced in the moment – the Salsa Trail is one.

Let's tie it all together...

The following is a piece I wrote called 'Kaha Lani: A Heavenly Place' (*Oro Valley-Marana* magazine, July 2008) about the Hawaiian island of Kauai. The purpose was to introduce the reader to the island with an overview of the island's setting, history and culture. The length was 400 words.

The introduction makes an effort to bring the reader to the island:

The ocean's breeze danced with the palm trees framing the balcony's beach view while the rainbow of roosters roaming the Kaha Lani Resort crowed as the sun crept up from the water.

Note that this passage delivers three senses: touch (the breeze coming from the ocean), sight (the wafting palm trees, the rainbow of roosters and the sunrise) and sound (the roosters crowing).

The next lines transition the piece into the informative section of the article:

Kaha lani (heavenly place) easily describes the six-million-year-old Hawaiian Island of Kauai. It's called the 'Garden Isle' for good reason. Only three per cent of its lush tropical landscape is developed for commercial and residential use. The remaining land nurtures acres of crops while the untamed sections provide natural playgrounds for the adventurous. Explorers can trek through thick tropical brush, swim beneath secluded waterfalls and soar through the treetops on zip-lines. Those charmed by the sea have their choice of adventures above and below the water or they can just lie back enjoy over 50 miles of white sand beaches.

The article then resumes, covering the island's sugar cane history and other island features:

> *The Nounou Mountain ridge, called the 'Sleeping Giant', is the backdrop for east Kauai and the subject of many island myths. The mountain range overlooks the Wailua River, the only navigable river in Hawaii and a gem for kayakers, motorboats, water skiers and the curious, with highlights such as the Fern Grotto, a natural lava-rock cave concealed in a rainforest and draped with ferns and a trickling waterfall descending from above. The area was once reserved for Hawaiian royalty but today riverboat cruises take passengers on a leisurely ride to the grotto with stories of folklore, hula dancers and Hawaiian chants.*

For the ending...

> *North of the river (note the transition), a short drive up Kuamo'o Road, are spectacular viewing areas of the river, Makaleha Mountains and the cascading Opaeka'a Falls – a kaha lani indeed.*

Focus points

Use an outline to guide your article or story.

Catch the reader's attention with an interesting, eye-catching lead. Usually this is the lead you used in your query to attract the editor's interest.

Offer an insightful main body of your article with appealing descriptions, interesting subheadings and facts.

Close with an interesting quote or final thought that sums up your article's purpose.

Use transitions for a smooth timeline.

Next step

Now that you know how to develop an article, it's time to learn how to launch, promote and make money running your own blog and cash-in on other blogging opportunities.

Blogging

In this chapter you will learn:

- ▶ *The pro and cons of blogging*
- ▶ *How to promote your blog*
- ▶ *Options for making money blogging*
- ▶ *How to brand your blog*

Blogging is self-employed travel writing at its finest. If you don't mind not having a pay cheque, at least at the beginning, blogging represents a fantastic opportunity. A small investment in your personal blog can open up a world that lets you take travel writing where you want, and allows you to be as creative as you desire. In fact, nearly every published travel writer I know owns or contributes to a blog.

That's not to say that blogging is for everyone. There is plenty of controversy over this craze and for good reason. Blogging can be compared to the fast food of today's writing world because posts can be written and published quickly. Unless you're blogging for a publication you are your own editor, publisher, marketing and finance crew.

Blogs and websites – what is the difference?

Before we start, let's decipher the difference between a weblog (blog) and a website. This is a common confusion.

Websites in the travel genera are either a personal website or a commercial website. An information-based website offers informative content and may offer travel services such as hotel, airline, rental car or cruise reservations. The pages usually fall under titled headings and are organized according to topic. Generally speaking, most websites aren't designed as an interactive platform with reader comment options, but you may have the opportunity to purchase or order products or services.

A blog, derived from the term 'weblog', is also a website but its format is different than a traditional website. A blog may also be part of a larger entity or stand alone. The entries, called blog posts, are usually dated and are featured in order, from the most recently posted back, while a website offers permanent articles. The content is usually written in non-formal, first-person journal style. Most blogs provide comment space for readers which allows for interaction between the writer and readers.

Carrie Finley-Bajak, editor of CruiseBuzz.net, describes the advantages of blogs:

> 'The best place to house content is a blog. Beginners can start with a free WordPress site and then transition to a hosted domain plan. The framework of the blog site needs to reflect your travel niche and in turn writers can take that content and give it new legs by syndicating the content across multiple channels. The goal is to generate traffic back to your website that either motivates readers to purchase your work, or to respond to a call to action like leaving a comment.'

Not everyone produces a high-quality blog, but if you make the effort, possess a decent dose of creativity and know how to pounce when you see an opportunity, you can do it. In this day and age, there's a new question to be asked of today's successful travel writers: What came first, travel writing or travel blogging?

Before we talk blogs, we need to get one thing straight. Like everything else in life, the blogosphere is evolving. But it's not slowly changing, it's rapidly morphing into something that we have yet to predict. For a few years, we had no idea what direction this new phenomenon was taking. Would it crash and burn or soar past the moon? The answer – at this moment – is both. Coming from a journalist perspective, just because everyone can blog, doesn't mean everyone should, and as time progresses and search engines change their tactics, only the strongest and most competitive will survive.

Dave Bouskill and Deb Corbeil, of ThePlanetD.com still think it is a worthwhile endeavour for the aspiring travel writer though:

> 'Success takes time and you may see people soaring past who are doing better than you, but don't compare yourself. If you stay true to your passion and have a solid vision of your brand, you will eventually find an audience. Make sure to read several travel blogs to learn and be inspired, but at the same time don't copy what others are doing. It's important to build a community to support one another and grow together.'

What makes a successful blog?

Unless you don't care about having an audience, meaning you're only writing about your travels for your immediate family, there are a number of points to check off your list. Much like launching a successful writing career, there's not really any secrets to doing the same for your travel blog. But there are some basic necessities every travel blog needs to follow:

▶ **Valuable content:** If your blog lacks worthy content and is riddled with poor grammar and typos, forget about it. A travel blog must be full of substance and polished to a shine.

▶ **Quantity:** It takes a while to build an index of blog posts; therefore keeping a writing schedule is paramount in building your blogging empire. Throwing in a little SEO (search engine optimization) won't hurt either. You need to be found in the search engines, but don't sacrifice your blog posts for SEO either. Good bloggers know how to massage their posts gently using SEO. Jennifer Miner of TheVacationGals.com says, 'Travel writing for online sites is, of course, somewhat different than the long, rambling narratives we expect to see in glossy travel magazines. While the personal narrative style – the art of travel blogging – is more creatively satisfying, new readers are generally found through online searches for particular topics (such as "where to go for a summer vacation"). Service pieces are more search engine optimized, and SEO – part of the business of travel blogging – is integral to being discovered and read by new readers online. Most of the successful travel blogs integrate SEO into their service-oriented posts, and leave room for more beautifully crafted travel posts to be simply that; writerly, well-written and fun to read.'

▶ **Audience appeal:** Travel bloggers should be able to answer the question: Who is your audience? And the blog posts must be written with readers in mind. This in turn will produce eyeballs which makes your blog increase in value.

▶ **Promotion:** As painful as it may be, marketing your blog is a must-do in order to catch reader eyes. This is where social media comes in (see Chapter 10).

▶ **Pretty:** Not every good blog will win a design award, but you do need to make sure the colours, text and appearance makes your posts easy to read. For example, if a website has a black background and white text I don't stick around to read it. It hurts my eyes. Appeal to the masses as you plan your blog layout.

BEWARE OF TYPOS:

As editor, if you're not careful, blogging can allow errors and typos to easily creep through. Just yesterday I was surfing a number of blogs and every single post on the various blogs had silly typos and grammar mistakes. Try your best to produce your best and if mistakes ever do creep in, correct them if you can, learn from your mistake and move on.

NO TRAVEL WRITING EXPERIENCE NEEDED

Don't think you have to be a published travel writer to launch your own blog. Dave Bouskill and Deb Corbeil of ThePlanetD. com are proof. The long-time married couple were freelancers in the film business, Dave was a rigging gaffer (head of lighting department) and Deb was a make-up artist. Every year they took several months to travel:

> 'After spending five years of splitting our time between work and travel, we decided that we wanted to turn our passion for seeing the world into a full-time career. We looked into several different ways of making a living out of travelling, from running tours, to becoming dive masters and eventually we decided that we wanted to pitch a travel show. We decided that we needed something epic to help us stand out in the travel world, so we signed up for the Tour d'Afrique, the world's longest cycling race from Cairo to Cape Town. Through this we gained a lot of publicity writing a series for a national newspaper in Canada and we made several TV appearances. We were asked if we would start a blog to chronicle the race for the Tour d'Afrique, so that is when ThePlanetD.com was born. It was mostly to support our trip through Africa and to be used as a place for potential employers to check out our videos, travel articles and experiences. Our travel

show never took off, but our website thrived. Deb took a travel writing course at a community college in Toronto and Dave took his extensive knowledge of lighting feature films and long time love of photography to turn it into a career. We then decided to focus on our travel blog and have never looked back.'

What is blogging exactly? It's storytelling, sharing thoughts, experiences, opinions and rants. It's helpful, fun and interactive. As Dave and Deb of ThePlanetD.com say, 'It is important to let your own voice and personality shine through no matter what you are writing about.'

Remember this

'Build your portfolio by starting your own blog. Expand it by guest blogging for others and commenting on travel websites – and plug your blog. Create a brand for yourself, find a niche and stick with it. Most of all, have fun!'

Benét J. Wilson, AviationQueen.com.

Blogger and boss

Erik Deckers is a travel blogger for the Indiana Department of Tourism, as well as a professional blogger (problogservice.com) and co-author of *Branding Yourself* and *No Bullshit Social Media* (2011)

> *'I think blogging is important for anyone who wants to break into travel writing. For one thing, it gives you a chance to develop your own voice and style without worrying about meeting the expectations of an editor.'*

Don't forget you're also taking on a lot of obligations. When you run your own blog you are the all-in-one editor, publisher, marketer and finance crew. That's why it's best to start slowly and don't try and do too much too soon. You can easily turn blogging into a 24-hour job and burn out before your efforts pay off. As the finance manager you need to know how much you can afford to invest and continue to put into your site.

Case study: Blogging and networking

Darren Cronian has been blogging since April 2005; he built a high-profile blog before Twitter and Facebook came on to the scene – but has since used the following tools to help him increase his audience and interact with them.

'Networking is about building relationships – without spending quality time networking I would never have achieved what I have in the time I have been writing about the travel industry. Networking led me to being interviewed on the TV and radio, and helped me create a blog that at its peak was attracting over 100,000 visitors a month.

When I started writing about travel consumer issues in April 2005 on the travelrants.co.uk blog, remember that Twitter did not exist and Facebook was just appearing on the horizon – so I spent time, every day, participating in discussions on blogs, forums and commented on articles on high-profile travel websites.

I split networking down into three groups: (1) networking with readers to build a community; (2) networking with journalists and writers; and (3) networking with potential clients and collaborators.

So what's the benefit of networking?

1 **Networking with readers to build a community:** Identify popular blogs and forums where you can add a link either in the forum signature, or in a blog comment section, this allows people to visit your blog. Firstly, you have to hook them in by writing a quality comment, hopefully they will take the hook – enjoy reading your blog and becomes a regular reader and a valuable member of your community who participates.

2 **Networking with journalists and writers:** the saying is true; it is not always what you know, but who you know. By leaving informative and thought provoking comments it helps you increase your authority in the niche you write about – I found that well-written comments attracted the attention of journalists and writers whose websites I was commenting on.

Over a period of time you start to build a relationship – this results in them writing about your blog and linking to it – the links help with search engine optimization – by building yourself into an authority, you will find journalists will contact you asking for quotes, which they publish in national newspapers, which attracts new readers.

Networking with people opens doors – in November 2008, I organized the TravelBlogCamp.co.uk, where I brought bloggers and travel companies together. This event is now in its fifth year, and is one of the more popular events at the World Travel Market in London – it's profitable too – and this is down to the fact that I spent time networking with travel companies that now sponsor the event.

3 **Networking with potential clients and collaborators:** Most of my time nowadays is spent working on my publishing business, creating Yorkshire guides (MyLifeinYorkshire.co.uk) that are written by local people, and rely partly on advertising to generate revenue; so networking with local businesses is an essential part of what I do.

Nowadays, I use social networks like Twitter to build a relationship. I ask them questions, show that I am passionate about the county, make them aware I know what I am talking about – help them. It makes it so much easier to approach them and arrange a meeting to discuss business or potential collaboration.

I still struggle to this day to network offline, but my one tip would be to find a small networking group near where you live, speak to at least one person, ask them questions about their business and tell them about yours, then build your confidence over time by speaking with more people.'

The blogger media kit

As a blog owner, displaying a media kit on your site is imperative. A media kit allows advertisers and PR professionals the opportunity to learn about you without taking any of your precious time.

As you develop your media kit, include these basics at the beginning then develop and update as needed:

➤ **A paragraph about you:** Explain why you're writing the blog.

- **Your topic:** What can readers expect your blog to cover?

- **Your market:** Who reads your blog? What group do your posts appeal to – mums, dads, young adults, seniors?

- **Stats:** There are several site counters for monitoring your site's progress. Google Analytics is one of the most popular. Some PR professionals ask for your Compete, Alexa and Quantcast ratings, but keep in mind that these aren't 100 per cent reliable.

- **Blog advertising rates:** Blogs have a number of revenue options. Advertisers will want to know how much you charge for: display ads, sponsored posts, text links, product reviews and giveaways. Ad space can be charged weekly, monthly and yearly. Conducting good business includes offering advertisers a discount for longer advertising periods. Make advertising with your blog beneficial and affordable yet competitive.

- **Speaking and writing rates:** Another perk of having your own job is writing and blogging assignments and speaking gigs will come to you seeking your expertise.

- **Media mentions:** Collect your blog's media references or awards relating to your blog. TV appearances, newspaper quotes, magazine references or any mention of you or your blog enhances your credibility and increases your value. Include links, scans or screenshots of your mentions.

- **Your clips:** If you used your blog to be published in other outlets, tell the world.

- **Your blog's social networking sites:** Include your links to Twitter, LinkedIn, Facebook, Pinterest, Google+, YouTube, Flicker, or any other social media site that you're active on. If you don't update regularly, leave it off.

- **Contact info:** Not only should you include your email address but consider including your phone number and list your given name for your contact information.

- **Headshot:** There are two reasons to keep a headshot in your media kit. First, it lets your future advertisers know you're a real person. Seeing someone's face gives people a sense of trust, whereas no photo keeps them wondering. Secondly, if you are quoted in the media, it's easy for a publication to find a photo of you to use (with your permission of course).

How to make money blogging

You work hard on your blog – now make it work for you by using your blog as leverage to writing for other publications. Put your web surfing skills to work by searching for holes in other publications then introduce your blog brand to larger, yet similar themed publications or publications lacking a section with your subject matter.

Of course, your blog can bring in money directly. Banner advertising, paid links, sponsored posts and affiliate programmes are a few ways travel bloggers make money off their blogs but there are other ways to do it, too.

Jennifer Miner (Jendeavor.com) also says online writing, and particularly blogging, is more important now than ever. 'Almost no one supports themselves solely by writing a travel blog; a travel blog is more typically a platform that leads to other freelance work. However, even a professional travel blog can be lucrative in terms of ongoing partnerships with CVBs (convention and visitors boards) and tourism companies, sponsorships and other online gigs. The barrier to entry is incredibly low (unless a new blogger wants to own his or her domain right away, it's free to start a blog), the learning curve sharp, and the potential enormous. What's not to like?'

MORE THAN MONEY

Another benefit of owning your own blog is the opportunity to be creative in how you are compensated. Over the years our blog has formed various partnerships with companies. We've exchanged gear and products for review. One luggage company signed with us for an entire year to review various pieces of their luggage line. The high-quality pieces made for easy and fun reviews.

How to write a review

If every review you write is glowing, people will question your authenticity. That's why it's imperative you give an honest review by sharing the positives and the negatives. As I tell my kids, it's not always what you say but how you say it that matters.

While you're describing a destination or piece of travel gear, explain what you like about it and what you would change if you could. Perhaps you visit the Arizona desert in the summer. It's hot and miserable, but you know that in six months snowbirds will be abandoning their colder regions for the lovely winter. Don't mislead by ignoring the heat. The desert heat actually makes for some good 'hot as a blow-torch' jokes. But also, focus on the benefits of visiting during the summer: dirt-cheap tee times at the golf courses, inexpensive hotels and lack of crowds.

Try it now

Write a 300–500 word review of a destination you've visited lately. Recall the senses you experienced (sights, sounds, smells and any details that can be described) and bring them to the reader through your descriptions. Next, what would you like to change? Was the location expensive, was the weather miserable or was it too crowded? Work that into your piece. Intrigue your audience by explaining the good and bad. Readers appreciate honestly.

After you write your piece, let it sit for a few days, then revisit it to rewrite and edit. When you feel good about your piece post it on your blog or, if you don't have a blog of your own yet, submit it to one of the many blogs that do accept guest posts. A quick search on Google for 'guest posts travel' will reveal lists of blogs open to guest writers. Be sure to read the site's blogger guidelines before submitting.

How not to promote your blog

When you first launch your blog you will be beyond ecstatic. And who can blame you? New adventures are always exciting. However, there are some things to keep in mind when you first start. Here are a few "don'ts" when you're just getting started:

Don't launch too soon. Ensure your pages are organized, images are sharp, content is coherent and links to other websites are correct.

Don't fill your entire social media pages or send private messages that are the same or similar to 'read my blog' posts. This is considered spam and will turn off any potential readership you may have otherwise attracted.

Don't seek sponsorship or advertisements until your numbers are competitive with other blogs similar to yours.

Don't expect overnight success. Take one day at a time. There is no such thing as instant success. A lot of time and effort goes into building a solid blog platform.

Don't quit. It takes time to build an audience and every day your numbers should grow. Hang in there and before long your blog will be thriving.

On the flip-side, there are some things you can do to increase your chances for success...

Ways to promote your blog

Owning a blog means you need to constantly be promoting and pushing your brand. It's no easy feat. Sometimes being a good writer just isn't enough. The competition is fierce in the blogosphere.

For years many blogs have survived by using the SEO tactic. But as the internet, and Google, evolve that method may soon be a ploy of the past. In the meantime, as long as it works still use it. You can find popular words and phrases via adwords.google. com. Besides SEO, here other ways to attract and keep readers:

▶ Offer giveaways of travel gear or other travel related items.

▶ Comment on influential travel blogs and include a link to your site.

- ▶ Post and keep relevant conversations going on social media.

- ▶ Promote others blogs, write about other bloggers and engage like-minded people on Facebook and Twitter.

Case study: branding your blog

Keith Jenkins is the founder and publisher of VelvetEscape.com, a luxury travel blog. Based in Amsterdam, he has visited more than 60 countries across six continents and writes about his travels on his Velvet Escape blog and exhibits his photos on The Happy Explorer.com photo blog. In addition to being a travel blogger, Keith often speaks at travel and social media conferences, and offers social media consultancy and marketing services via his Velvet Connect and iambassador brands. He is also the co-founder of the Global Bloggers Network, a community that helps individual and corporate travel bloggers grow and monetize their blogs. Follow Keith on Twitter: @velvetescape.

'Branding is an important element to consider when one starts a blog. An appealing, clearly defined brand can be a pivotal contributor to the success of a blog, helping to drive traffic, create a community around the blog and ease monetizing efforts.

What makes a brand stick? A beautiful, professionally-designed logo is not sufficient. A blog's brand consists of a number of building blocks; aside from the logo, these include the online personality of the blogger, the blogger's preferred travel style, the 'story' behind the blog, the look-and-feel of the blog and the content. The key to creating a successful brand is to get these blocks to merge seamlessly and portray the same message. In this sense, consistency is paramount.

▶ Domain name

Building a blog brand starts with claiming the domain name and self-hosting your blog. Self-hosting is crucial for a variety of reasons. It allows for greater flexibility in the set-up and layout of the blog, exudes greater professionalism but most importantly, your brand is given the centre-stage in the URL field (e.g. 'velvetescape.com' as opposed to 'velvetescape.wordpress.com'). This in turn helps search engines to easily identify and index your blog and propel your brand to number one in search results.

▶ Logo and tagline

The logo and tagline of your blog is another important building block of your brand. A simple, eye-catching logo works best. Pay special attention to the colours used in the logo and try to utilize these subtly in other areas of your blog (e.g. bullets and linked text). The colours represent your brand. Using the same colour in text bullets in your posts or sub-headers in your sidebar promotes brand visibility in other parts of your blog and creates an aura of uniformity.

A tagline is equally important. When a reader visits your blog for the first time, the logo is a visual/pictoral form of identity whilst the tagline gives readers a quick hint about the tone of the blog and what it's about. Keep you tagline short and snappy. Be creative!

▶ Look and feel

Your logo and tagline are one of the first things readers see when they visit your blog. As they scroll down, a clean, attractive look-and-feel will make them stay longer whilst a clear navigation makes it easier for them to explore other parts of the blog. A consistent look-and-feel is another important element of your brand. Use your house colors, headers and sub-headers, adequate spacing and size and positioning of photos to transmit a consistent message across all pages of your blog.

▶ Personality

The personality of the person behind the blog is the most prominent element of a blog's brand. Readers return to blogs more often if they easily identify with or simply like the blogger. There are various ways to create an appealing online personality. Having a compelling story in your 'About' page helps (e.g. investment banker quits his job, travels around the world, discovers a passion for travel blogging and makes a career out of it). The same goes for having a clear description of your interests and preferred ways to travel. An attractive profile photo can also work wonders. In addition, finding your 'voice', or rather, a writing style that effectively projects your personality to your readers, is pivotal in creating a unique brand.

As unique content becomes increasingly challenging to create, the personality of the blogger and his/her style become more important in differentiating the blog from the rest. In this sense, whilst content is (and should always be) the main focus, personality and style are the cornerstones of the blog's brand.

▶ Content

Content is the voice of your brand. People visit your blog to read what you have to say. Quite often, it's not what is being said but rather how it's said that makes people stay and keeps them engaged. Hence, it is important to inject sufficient amounts of your personality into your content. Using your personality and style effectively can bring the most mundane topic to life while enthusing your readers.

Always keep in mind that your content should reflect your brand. It is therefore important that the topics you choose to write about and the way you write it remains consistent with your brand message.

▶ Your readers and colleagues

A blog's brand is largely created by the blogger. However, you can also involve your readers and blogger colleagues to help you develop and/or strengthen your brand. As an example, I often ask my readers or fellow bloggers to think of what the name 'Velvet Escape' means to them and where they can find this in their hometown. The result is a guest post series called 'My Velvet Escape travel tip'. This branding exercise has helped to create awareness of the brand by getting people to think about and write about it. More importantly, readers associate the activity (the 'Velvet Escape') with the brand and this allows them to experience it first-hand.

These are the main building blocks which are required to create a brand. It's a lot of fun putting these blocks together and it's a great test of your creativity. Once you have the blocks up, review the various elements regularly and make appropriate adjustments. In addition, find new ways to raise your brand awareness and visibility.

Have fun – if you're having fun, so will your readers! And remember, consistency is key.'

DON'T SPREAD YOURSELF TOO THIN

The travel writing and blogging world offers something exciting to do on every corner – from guest posts to launching a second or third blog. One of the problems that writers face is taking on too many projects. This is especially true in the blog realm. Before you start a second blog, focus on the one you have and make sure it can stand on its own before you start a new project or agree to contribute to other blogs.

STRENGTH IN NUMBERS

Having multi-bloggers can be beneficial for everyone involved. In my personal experience, as a mother with a full-time job, it would have been very challenging for me to start and keep my own travel blog alone in addition to keeping up with my freelance assignments. That's not to say that having a group blog is ideal for everyone. Sharing a blog has its benefits and its downfalls.

Benefits:

- You can draw from different people's experience.
- Blog posts will offer a variety of opinions, experiences and voices.
- Using everyone's talents might create something fantastic.
- You can assign duties (respond to email, run finances, manage advertising).
- There is usually always someone available to handle any crisis.
- You don't have to post as frequently.

Drawbacks:

- Too many cooks … conflicts can arise due to different thoughts and opinions on how the blog should be run.
- Some people end up doing more work than others.
- You have to share the proceeds.
- Your writing schedules can conflict.

If you aren't web savvy, then consider hiring someone who is to manage the techie details. College kids to stay-home-mums run their own affordable web businesses.

Case study: blogging

What does it take to break into travel writing?

Liz Lewis is a freelance travel, health and lifestyle writer. Having lived in various places in the world (Hawaii, Crete, California, Germany and Saudi Arabia), Liz now resides in New Zealand.

'Six years ago, long before everyone and their dog had a travel blog, I decided that I wanted to be a travel writer. At the time, I had no idea how to go about it. I had no writing experience. I had no contacts. I had no plan. And worse yet, I lived in New Zealand – about as far away from the main travel writing industry as you could possibly can get.

So I did what I always do whenever I come up with an off-the-wall idea, I simply jumped in feet first and hoped for the best. I started by reading, and reading, and then reading some more. Mostly I read hardcopy books by travel writers about travel writing.

I learned about query letters and pitches, about how to analyze magazines, and why you should never send an editor a finished article on spec. Buoyant with all this knowledge, I pitched and I pitched and I pitched some more and got nowhere.

New Zealand markets, it turned out, were impossible to crack and the United States markets were too far away. I was just about ready to quit. Then I discovered the joys of travel blogging.

No more pitching, no more rejection letters, no more editors who couldn't remember my name. With travel blogging, I could write what I liked. I could, in fact, be in charge of my own destiny as a travel writer. All I had to do was build a travel blog. But building a travel blog doesn't guarantee a readership. So I started reading again, this time travel blogs, good and bad. And along the way, I came to the conclusion that there are basically five essential ingredients to any good travel blog.

1 **Make it interesting.** Nobody, possibly not even your mother, is interested in reading an itinerary. Create a living, breathing blog. After all, you're writing about travel here and there is nothing more alive than travel. Share anecdotes. Explain why a place is worth visiting. Be descriptive – focus on colours, the smells, the sounds and the music.

2 **Be informative.** People read travel blogs to discover new places to visit or learn more about places they've been or want to go. So share the knowledge. Tell them how to get there, inform them about festivals, costs, accommodation and transportation. Give them the true scoop on a place, warts and all.

3 **Use dynamic visuals.** Photographs talk. Post photographs that will make reader's mouth water, stimulate their senses, and make them feel that they are there with you.

4 **Entertain your readers.** Share your travel anecdotes. If you get blisters walking the trails of the Grand Canyon, ate grubs at a wild food festival, and drove a Cadillac along Route 66 share the experience. Make the readers laugh out loud. Help them hear the music.

5 **Post consistently.** Let your readers know when and how often you are going to post. The more you blog, the more likely the readers will stick around. If you're only going to blog once or twice a week, tell the readers. If you're taking a break from blogging while you're on the road, let them know when you'll be back.

To help out, here are some key words to focus on when writing your travel blog:

T – Tantalizing Tempting Thrilling Timely Tremendous Truthful

R – Reliable Regular Radiant Real Refreshing Remarkable Responsible

A – Appealing Absorbing Adventurous Amusing Atmospheric Authentic

V – Visual Vibrant Vocal Valuable Valid

E – Enthralling Entertaining Eloquent Energetic Enjoyable Enticing

L – Lively Leading Liberating Limitless Loaded

So six years on, I consider myself a travel writer. It's never going to make me rich, at least not monetarily. But by being able to share my travel stories with others, it makes me a richer person.

Have a purpose

When venturing into the wild world of blogging, it's important to recognize your intention. Dave Bouskill and Deb Corbeil of Planet D say that identifying your purpose will help you develop your blog: 'Do you want to be a professional blogger or is it simply a platform for family and friends to follow your round the world trip. If a career is your choice, be prepared to put in a lot of work.'

There are also challenges to such a lifestyle. Disconnecting from friends and family is the hardest part of travel blogging:

> 'As the years pass, we are starting to lose our connection with long time friends and even feel distant from our families. Their lives have gone on without us and when we come home, we aren't the first people on their minds. When we first started travelling, people were excited when we returned home, but now understandably it is old hat. It can be difficult to integrate back into people's lives. We all still care about one another, we are just travelling different paths in life right now.

Benefits of guest blogging

Marketing strategies are not limited to selling products or services, it also pertains to your blog and how you promote it. Link exchanges, blog rolls and comment circles (posting comments on each other's blogs so it appears you have an active audience) have been hot-topics within the blogosphere. The other popular trend is guest blogging which is simply writing for other websites.

There are many benefits to contributing to other blogs. You will get links back to your own blog or website which can attract traffic and boost your Google page rank. You should also be offered a bio that accompanies your work that gives you exposure and if the blog is respectable you will gain credibility and can add it to your list of writing credits.

!

Focus points

Have a vision and purpose for your blog.

Blogging is more than writing: it's a business.

Think of your blog as a brand.

Develop a media kit and update it often.

Get creative in your blogging income opportunities.

Next step

Blogging is the foundation for the travel writer's platform today, but it's just a portion of getting your name out there and into an editor's rolodex. Chapter 10 is about social media and the power of networking, and explores how Web 2.0 can assist your travel writing career.

Social Media and Travel Writing

In this chapter you will learn:

- ► *How to use social media to boost your travel-writing career*
- ► *The best social media platforms for writers*
- ► *How to find editors and other travel writers online*
- ► *How to network through social media*
- ► *How to use photography in social media*

Facebook, Twitter, Pinterest, YouTube have become entities of their own as well as outlets for travel writers. Travel writers can use the benefits of these platforms for self-promotion, connecting with editors and receiving invitations for press trips. It is a great way to take a break from work, makes for easy online networking, allows writers to find and connect with other like-minded people and often leads to writers finding assignments.

Social media has changed the way we communicate and it's certainly made an impact on the new wave of travel writing. The social media world is comparable to a live, 24-hour TV travel channel. There is always a story or adventure to tune into anytime you log on and in every facet you desire. Depending upon your niche you will likely find your channel, tune in and possibly stay there.

Professional benefits of social media

Every social media platform has its own vibe and you shouldn't discredit any of them. Twitter is the social and promotional scene. Facebook is what you make of it with the choice of business or personal. LinkedIn is primarily professional.

Let's take a quick look at each of these more closely, since these are the most popular social media networking forums.

TWITTER
Twitter is constantly evolving but is considered a social, promotional and networking scene. I've been a member since 2008 and have learned a few tricks for keeping my Twitter use in balance:

▶ **Search hashtags:** To keep up with industry news look for Tweets tagged with the themes you like to follow: #travel, #airlines, #flying, #familytravel, #writers are just a few that I like to check in on every day. Depending up on your niche, yours will be a little different.

▶ **Keep lists.** I keep several lists to keep organized. You can share your lists with your followers or keep them private. Some of my public and private lists include Minnesota, airlines/aviation, travel, writers and, my favourite, people I've met IRL (in real life).

▶ **Connect with your audience, editors and other writers:** Twitter allows you to build your own personal community. Choosing people with the same topic interests will give you a place to share and learn.

▶ **Limit your time on Twitter:** It's okay not to be on Twitter 24/7. Twitter allows members to get instant notifications if someone DMs (direct message) you or mentions your handle. Don't give anyone the power to distract you from your work. Turn your alerts off and limit the time you spend on Twitter. Being that I'm an extrovert it's easy for me to get sucked into the social media world. I could stay on all day chatting it up with people. Instead, I allow myself to check in when I'm taking a break from writing, such as drinking my morning coffee, eating lunch or between flights.

▶ **Use your timeline for travel:** Tweet your travel experiences, share photos, voice your thoughts, retweet others and offer helpful travel tips.

FACEBOOK

Fortunately, Facebook is evolving to allow users to keep work and personal lives separate. Carrie Finley-Bajak, editor of CruiseBuzz.net says:

'Facebook is a great platform for interacting with friends. Consider setting up a fan page for your brand and don't be shy about interacting with other travel writers or colleagues. The goal is to be active, social and reinforce your expertise on your subject.'

Consider Facebook as a gathering place to bond with other travel writers, promote yourself and show off your adventures.

Remember this

The most successful people are busy working behind the scenes and pop in only during breaks or when their work is finished and in most cases no one even notices they were gone. Work first, socialize later. Social media is always there.

LINKEDIN FOR ASSIGNMENTS

If someone is curious about your professional background they will likely visit your LinkedIn page. Profiles feature work history, current projects, schooling, awards and recommendations. Users can actually keyword their profile so it's more likely to appear in searches, share their career goals and receive recommendations from peers or other professionals.

When you invite others to connect, introduce yourself and share how you know each other. LinkedIn users are more picky about who they connect with since this platform is used for actual professional networking. If you have not met, explain why you want to connect. This is not the network for collecting random friends.

Everyone I know has had a different experience with LinkedIn. Personally, I've had wonderful success connecting with others. The various groups are helpful for asking and answering questions as well as uniting with other likeminded people on current events, upcoming gathers and, yes, even scoring assignments.

It was through LinkedIn that I was approached by an editor to write for an aviation trade magazine. I've now contributed five feature pieces (all over 2,000 words) to the publication. Not only did I land a fantastic writing opportunity that I enjoyed, I'm able to use these articles as fodder for my professional resumé since the topic is in my field.

Some tips for making your profile more attractive to editors or other members searching for someone in your field include:

- ▶ Keyword your profile.

- ▶ Connect with people in your field.

- ▶ Update your profile often.

- ▶ Participate in groups, answer questions and start conversations.

The balancing act

As I touched on earlier, despite the necessity of social media, there needs to be a balance when it comes to online socializing. Social media can be a time suck. As you enter the travel writing world, you will find that many people, in all fields, choose to spend most of their day socializing online rather than working. It's no surprise these people then complain about not being able to find work, time to work, or are missing deadlines.

Some social media platforms such as Hootsuite or TweetDeck allow users to schedule updates while you're travelling or away from the computer.

RIDICULOUS DISTRACTIONS

Twitter has been compared to social gatherings on many occasions, there's even a book called *Social Media is a Cocktail Party* (CreateSpace, 2008) by Jim Tobin and Lisa Braziel. If we were to all ditch our jobs and unite at a cocktail party 24 hours a day, we wouldn't get much done. Keep this analogy in the forefront of your mind the next time you log on to your favourite social media sites.

Don't get obsessed with 'best of...' lists that feature the 'top' people in social media, social media 'scores' or voting contests that don't determine anything other than who could garner the most votes from friends and families. Many of these silly lists and contests drifting across the social media scenes are designed to bring page views to the host's websites. Note: occasionally, there are some authentic lists and voting opportunities that are worthy, but these are usually hosted by professional PR firms who are selective while pulling the lists they compile and it certainly is an honour to be listed. But for the most part, don't get upset if your name isn't on a list.

Don't get wrapped up in the drama. That's supposed to be something we left behind in high school. However, social media has a way of highlighting commotion and trends, from Hollywood stars to politics. Try to avoid pointless conversations and arguments that are non-productive.

Don't linger. If you're easily sucked into the social media whirlwind for hours a day, that means you're behind hours a day in your career. Unless you've made a career out of social media such as being the face behind a corporate social media account or planning Twitter parties, social media doesn't pay for those of us who freelance or are our own brands. Instead, take Tim Leffel, travel writer, editor and author's advice:

> 'Treat social media like alcohol and recreational drugs. In moderation these self-affirmation tools can be useful: good social lubricants that expand your circle of friends. Over-indulge in them most of your workdays, however, and your job will suffer. There are usually much more productive uses of your time than Twitter or Facebook once you get

past the point of 5–15 minutes a day. (And this is coming from a guy who runs four websites and five blogs.) Spend most of your working time on things that will last, not on status updates that will be forgotten in a day.'

Forums

Themed forums and, even more popular today, Facebook pages, are an ideal way to connect with other people in your niche and in the travel writing world. You can ask and answer questions, connect with others going to the same conferences and press trips and get advice for visiting upcoming destinations. When you're new to the travel writing world, most of your questions can be answered in these forums or Facebook groups. Use the website's search tool to discover past conversations about the topics you're interested in. Before you know it, you'll be the expert leading they way for future travel writers.

Case study: social media

Sheila Scarborough is a writer and speaker specializing in tourism, travel and social communications. A Navy veteran and co-founder of TourismCurrents.com, she thinks everyone should have a passport and experience jet lag. She is also one of the authors of Perceptive Travel Blog (PerceptiveTravel.com/blog) and she runs a personal blog SheilasGuide.com.

'Make no mistake; social media is not going to overcome bad travel writing or lack of professionalism (not turning assignments in on time, not meeting your assigned word count, being way too hard to work with or the million other ways that people fail with the basics.)

The other important thing to remember is that, as I learned from motivational author and speaker Harvey Mackay, 'dig your well before you're thirsty'. Just like flailing to build career connections on LinkedIn AFTER you've been laid off reeks of desperation, trying to build online connections that you immediately spam with links to your stuff is going to get you ignored and/or blocked.

Where to get started? Go where the people are who might enjoy your travel stories. There's a big travel bloggers' Facebook group, gatherings like the Travel track at BlogWorld & New Media Expo, travel chats on Twitter like #TTOT and #TNI, or, if it's all too much, just the comments sections of some of your own favourite blogs are a fine place to begin meeting fellow travel enthusiasts.

Don't forget going 'old school' with things like adding your blog URL to your email signature, and contributing to forums (the Frommer's travel forum www.frommers.com/community/ has been going strong for years.) Add value and be helpful by answering questions about topics and regions where you have expertise. Your profile will have a link back to your blog or website; if people like what you say, they WILL click through to read more.

Give to get, and you'll be fine.

Focus points

Partake in social media and build online networks.

Don't let social media dominate your day, use it as an enhancement to your career.

Use online contacts for networking.

Set up your social media pages for self-promoting and to attract assignments.

Keep in touch with the people you meet in real life by checking in on social media.

Next step

Today's travel writer is often expected to not only be a wordsmith and social media savvy, but also capable of providing photography and videos with assignments. Chapter 11 will reveal the various formats to enhance your work.

Photography
and Videos

In this chapter you will learn:

► *Tips for shooting video and photography*
► *The importance of backing up your photography*
► *The benefits of vlogging*

Today's travel writer is often expected to not only be a wordsmith but also be capable of providing photography and videos with assignments. In fact, sometimes travel writers with savvy photography skills can break into a publication by offering their photos for slideshows accompanied by photo captions. This chapter will show the various formats to enhance your work including vlogging (video blogging).

To make it as a travel writer today you need to be as diverse as possible when it comes to the various multimedia options. Not every writer is a photographer and not every photographer is a writer, but learning to take photos can augment your personal blog's posts as well as your chances for publication. Huffington Post editor, Chris Anderson, explains:

> 'Travel writing isn't just writing. It is providing a complete and accurate experience, and I can't stress enough how important it is to not only paint a picture with your words, but to provide a visual element. It is easier than ever with technology. Good cameras are cheap, and even some great video if you're writing for web can enhance the package. As an editor in digital media, I definitely give preference to a writer who can provide the whole package and tell a complete story with a variety of media.'

The money shot

Unless your blog is all photos, you will need to be taking photos with your words in mind. Dave Bouskill and Deb Corbeil of ThePlanetD.com, who work together to create beautiful content, have the following advice:

> 'You will have to look at your travels from a story angle. Take photographs of everything, take notes on the places you visit and the sites you see and instead of heading out to the bar every night to party with your new travel companions, be prepared to work in your hotel room putting together blog posts and sharing your articles through your social media channels. You can still have a lot of fun while you travel, but you won't be on a permanent vacation.'

Back up

While we've already discussed the importance of backing up your written work, it's also important to do the same with your photos. I can't reiterate this enough. Let me explain why. It was 2008 and I was on a getaway with some of my writing girlfriends. We started out as a group in Maui and then were split up to explore additional islands. Naturally, my Nikon-80 had been getting a lot of action. I downloaded my photos onto my computer, labelled the file and admired my work which consisted of breathtaking sunsets, beachside luaus, lavender fields and glasses of pineapple wine.

Needing to make room on my camera for more photos I began deleting the photos after they were downloaded. After departing Maui, I went to Kauai for a couple of days taking hundreds more photos of waterfalls, sunrises and crowing roosters. After taking a red-eye to the mainland I popped open my computer to kill time between my final flight from Los Angeles to Tucson. As soon as I hit the power button I heard an awful screeching noise and saw a blank computer screen. The end result was a wiped-out hard drive. Only five photos and some of my documents were rescued. Luckily, I hadn't erased my Kauai photos from my camera.

I did land a print Kauai article assignment, but didn't have any luck selling my Maui stories because I didn't have any photos to accompany them. This was a hard lesson to learn but I'm grateful to be able to pass it on to my readers with hopes you never make this mistake.

Remember this

Never delete the photos from your camera until they are downloaded and backed up.

Vlogging

Some bloggers opt to include the video blogging (vlogging) medium on their sites. As Melanie Nelson of BloggingBasics101. com says of video blogging, 'It's a great way to take the relationship with your readers to another level.'

As video popularity continues to grow, jumping in front of the camera as a travel writer and sharing your surroundings with your readers-turned-viewers, is a great way to bring the destination to your audience. If you're uncomfortable in front of the camera, start with a few words of commentary or background on the area then step aside to reveal scenic views or interesting sights. A minute or two is all you need. Feel free to get creative. Creativity is on your side, write an entire blog post and include the video or only post the video.

Author and professional blogger Erik Deckers of ProBlogService.com advises writers to invest in a decent camera and post images and videos whenever possible:

> 'Upload them to a photo and video sharing site and embed this content onto your blog posts. Build up your network as large as you can, whether it's travel enthusiasts, people in your community and neighboring areas (if you want to be a 'local' travel writer), as well as travel and tourism professionals.'

Rick Griffin and Sandi McKenna, the producers and co-hosts of MidlifeRoadtrip.tv., have more advice:

> 'Shooting video on location is a lot different from shooting in a controlled studio environment. Because each location is different, extra planning and preparation are required to make sure you're able to get the shots you need to tell the story you want to tell. A storyboard provides the basic framework for your shot list and is especially important when shooting a travel video.'

The pair use four elements in their storyboards:

1 **Set the scene.** When shooting on location, it's important for your audience to know WHO and WHERE you are. We usually establish the scene with a wide-angle shot in the opening sequence.

2 **Set the action.** Establish WHY you are there. Let the audience know your purpose for being at that particular location.

3 **Next, it's showtime.** This is the big climactic part of the video where you do WHAT you came to do ... or at least attempt to do what you came to do.

4 **Last but not least – the wrap.** Where you tie it all together and explain HOW the experience made you feel.

> *A great tip for any location is to make sure you shoot LOTS of B-roll. B-roll is an editor's best friend, it's the footage that is used to support the story and break up long static shots. It also makes for a great band-aid for patching sequences and covering mistakes. Once you have your storyboard and know what you're going to shoot, it's time to gather the gear you'll need for making your video.*

McKenna and Griffin suggest packing extension cords and plenty of fully charged batteries and a battery operated camera light for poor lighting. The pair also says to be aware of background noises. A remote external microphone will come in handy for keeping the audio you want in the foreground:

> *'Another important piece of gear is a tripod. Without it, your video may look like you're in an earthquake. Be sure you've got a script, a shot list and a checklist. You want to make sure you have everything you need. Shooting a video without a script or all of your gear is like jumping out of a plane without a parachute.'*

After you have your video finished you will want to rely on editing software 'to make some magic happen' says the Midlife Roadtrip crew:

> *'Editing software allows you to take all of the footage you've shot and arrange it into a logical sequence. You can polish it up and make it look very professional by tweaking the sound and color, and adding graphics, titles, music and voice-overs.'*

Professional tips

Sometimes packing lots of gear isn't possible but you still want to be able to capture good footage. Award-winning video producer Dave Sniadak (HDHubby.com) of Minnesota offers a few pointers:

If you don't want to take the time to lug around a bulky tripod, you can use a few simple ways to help stabilize your camera. Consider leaning against a wall, your car or a railing or fence to steady your body as you try to capture the perfect shot. If you're shooting scenic shots out in the wide open and there's nothing to lean against, set the camera on your wallet, backpack or cooler to ensure maximum stability.

The one thing that made photographers like Ansel Adams and Eliot Porter so amazing was their ability to frame a shot that captured the emotion of the scene. Remember this simple phrase: HE-RO-COMP, short for 'Head Room and Composition'. If you're cutting off the top of your subjects' head or there's more sky above them than torso below, you'll want to adjust your shot. Additionally, look around your shot before clicking the shutter or pressing record.

Shoot judiciously but asking yourself: 'Will an editor be interested in this video? Will this picture really speak a thousand words?' If you answered no, question why you need to capture the moment. If there is a chance you will end up shooting two hours of video, but only ten minutes of that footage is something you'd be proud to share, you'll want to think before you press record.'

Case study: multimedia assignment adventures

Tim Shisler is a photo and video editor at Mountain News Corporation, but also has had his name in print. He offers his perspective on the combination of images and travel writing and shares one of his most memorable multimedia assignments:

'If you're a writer today there's no denying you'll be asked to shoot video, Tweet during the trip and take magazine-quality photos while you're doing everything else.

If you're a writer who has a point and shoot camera that's okay, but don't promote yourself as a professional photographer who can capture low-light scenes with the same level of craftsmanship that a photographer who has the proper equipment. Of course that by no means is an excuse not to shoot photos. Quite simply, if you're a writer and wanting to get into travel writing, make sure you can take decent photos, decent video and navigate social networks. Otherwise, you're going to have to be one of those rare writers who is just so damn good everything falls away.

The best adventure I had was for Catharine Hamm from the **Los Angeles Times**. *I first met Catharine while I was presenting to a group of editors about the value of online video and she approached me afterward with a simple proposition. 'We should talk,' she said and then got ambushed by a colleague. A few agonizing months later we connected and decided I would drive up through California and Oregon and report on four areas that were slated to potentially become National Monuments. The task was daunting – I had just three weeks to travel over 6,000 miles, shoot video, interview folks, take pictures, GPS parts of each region and come back and produce everything. Adding icing to the cake, my travel budget was $7 (£4 46) a day for food and I had enough money to spend one night in a hotel. Lugging around camera gear, camping gear, food and everything else got to be a challenge and the 100-degree heat throughout the trip didn't help either. But in the end it all worked out and taught me more about reporting, life and how to do all the different aspects of multimedia than if I had stayed home for the summer in Colorado. Catharine ended up putting the piece in a Sunday edition and even put my photos on the entire front page of the travel section. It wasn't always pretty, I had winged a majority of the trip and I vowed next time I do something like this I'll need a bigger budget, but the fact remains it was still an assignment I'll never forget and one that allowed me to take what I'd always been saying regarding multimedia and show I could actually pull it off. Without people like Catharine who gave me a chance I'd never really know what could have been.'*

Focus points

Today's travel writer sometimes needs to be able to produce solid photos or video in order to sell an article.

If you plan to run a travel blog or website images are a necessity.

If you plan to shoot video become familiar with your tools and practice at home before trying to produce something that's usable.

Don't push yourself as a professional photographer if you're not, but offer photos if you do have them.

Practise using photo editing on your photos. Sometimes a little brightening or cropping is all a photo needs.

→ **Next step**

While writing and photos go hand-in-hand in today's travel writing world, there's another factor that can help you land assignments more easily than ever and that is through networking. Chapter 12 is going to show you ways to make the most of your professional contacts and how to keep those relationships alive.

The Importance of Networking

In this chapter you will learn:

- ▶ *How to network efficiently*
- ▶ *The benefits of joining an organization*
- ▶ *Why it's 'who you know...'*
- ▶ *How to work with publicists*

Once you realize the magic of networking, your efforts will seem to magically take you where you need to go. As Tim Shisler, photo and video editor at Mountain News Corporation, says:

> *'The truth of the matter though is I didn't get started in this profession because I was necessarily more talented than others, but because I had a lot of people willing to take a chance on me and help me out. Without them I'd never have made it this far.'*

Many writers feel that they are not the best writers, but their perseverance and networking is what helped them climb the Mount Everest of travel writing. It's okay to let friends and acquaintances help you by offering recommendations or letting you name drop.

Chris Anderson of Huffington Post explains:

> *'Travel writing gives you a chance to connect with a wide range of people in powerful positions and the importance of networking while you travel and maintaining your relationships cannot be stressed enough, because you never know what opportunities might come up. And they will come up.'*

Help others

As you venture into the travel writing world, take the approach of helping others and they will in turn help you when the time comes. Travel writer Carolyn B. Heller says:

> *'Writing is a people business. Connect with other writers, introduce them to editors you meet, and don't hesitate to suggest another writer for an assignment. It's good karma and will help send leads back your way.'*

Case study: Network your way to paid writing gigs and press trips

Kara Williams of TheVacationGals.com has a knack for networking. Part of the reason is her natural inclination for helping others. If an editor approaches her with an assignment that she can't accept, she will happily offer names of others who may be able to take the assignment. Or, if a writer is looking for a source she's the first person to offer possible contacts. This in turn has brought her some fantastic opportunities.

Kara, who makes her home in the Colorado Rockies with her husband and two school-age children, writes about family travel, spas and outdoor adventures – not only in her home state, but also throughout North America, Mexico and the Caribbean. Learn more about her at karaswilliams.com.

'To a novice travel writer, networking might sound a little frightening. After all, you may feel like a small fish in a big pond of accomplished writers and influential public-relations professionals in the travel industry. But don't let the term 'networking' frighten you! It's not purely about perfecting your elevator pitch ('Hi, my name is Kara; I'm from Colorado, and I particularly like to write about family travel, spas and outdoor adventures in my own backyard and beyond...'), nor is it solely about handing out business cards left and right. To me, networking with other writers, editors and PR folks is about being friendly, approachable, and perhaps most important, willing to share your own tips, experiences and contacts. Yes, even those new to travel writing have valuable things to share! And trust me, the sooner you get out there letting people know that you're an active, enthusiastic travel writer, the sooner opportunities will come your way. Here's how:

✳ **Join online forums:** Invaluable to me when I started focusing on travel writing six years ago was the 'bulletin board' at Travelwriters. com. The site still exists, though participation on the board is nearly stalled these days, perhaps because of the advent of social media sites such as Twitter (see below) and travel-related Facebook groups. Today, I have met and become friendly with other travel writers at the online forums connected to FreelanceSuccess.com (designed for established writers; you can ask for a sample membership to check out the forums before committing to the $99/year fee) and TravelBlogExchange.com (free to join).

✳ **Join travel writing organizations:** Invaluable for my ongoing networking are my memberships in the American Society of Journalists and Authors (ASJA.org) and the Society of American Travel Writers (SATW.org). Both of these associations require a body of published articles in order to join, but once you get some clips under your belt, I highly recommend you look into both of these groups. They have online forums to chat with other members as well as annual conferences to meet up in real life. Other travel-writing organizations include North American Travel Journalists Association (NATJA.org), Midwest Travel Writers Association (MTWA.org) and International Food, Wine and Travel Writers Association (ifwtwa.org) – and that's just to name a few!

✳ **Join Twitter:** This microblogging site has been truly invaluable to me in connecting with others in the travel writing industry. Begin following some of your favourite travel brands, city CVBs or hotel chains. From there, you'll find public-relations professionals and travel writers who are also following these brands or destinations; follow them and your followers will in turn grow! From there, participate in travel-related Twitter chats (#tni, #luxchat, #ttot, #nuts, #cruisechat) and join the conversation! Sometimes travel writers or PR folks will broadcast some great travel opportunities. I saw a Miami-based travel PR exec announce she was looking for writers on a Caribbean press trip. I responded to her Tweet ASAP, and six weeks later found myself in Aruba.

✳ **Meet people in real life:** By attending Travel Media Showcase (travelmediashowcase.com) in Kansas City in 2008, I had drinks with a friendly website editor. A few months later he contacted me to write for a new blog he was starting; that lucrative steady gig lasted two-and-a-half years. I spoke at a digital media seminar for travel-related PR professionals in Denver; on the panel was a newspaper travel editor, for whom I promptly wrote a few hotel profiles and for whom I'm now writing a monthly travel column. I met a magazine editor on a press trip to Cancun, and have since written three articles for her. I could go on and on with stories such as this. It is so key to meet – and yes, exchange business cards with – others in the industry in person. In each of these instances, I'm certain that 'cold calling' these editors would not have resulted in steady, ongoing work. In this business, snagging great writing gigs is indeed about 'who you know' – whether that's someone you've met at a conference, had drinks with, played golf with or bantered with on Twitter.

✳ **Don't burn bridges:** You never know when someone you've worked with in your past can give you work in the future. Case in point: I worked on staff for three years at a tour operator, editing their weekly itineraries and doing other corporate copywriting for the worldwide company. When I left my full-time job, I was offered some work writing brochures on one of their new products; a great gig as I could do the work from my new home, four hours from the corporate office. Furthermore, when a huge online travel agency that sold those tours needed someone to help with their brochure and website copy, I was the recommended writer. That travel agency has been a steady, lucrative client for more than five years now! Always do your best work, always end a project or leave an office job on good terms, and I suspect more work will follow.

✻ **Share your contacts:** I can't stress enough how much I've seen karma work to my advantage in the travel-writing industry. I'm always happy to pass on PR contacts, editors' names and travel opportunities to others. It's a big, big world out there when it comes to travel writing, and I feel like the pie is large enough for us to all share it. Here's one example of putting goodness out there and having it come back to me: Recently I was asked to recommend travel writers for two huge travel opportunities I couldn't accept – an all-expenses paid trip to Hawaii and an all-expenses paid cruise. I happily shared more than a dozen contacts of writers I thought did great work, were social-media savvy and were all-around good people. Not 24 hours after I sent those emails with my travel-writer recommendations did a fellow SATW member (with whom I serve on an internal committee) recommend me to her editor of an in-flight magazine. That editor was looking for a Colorado based writer, and I happened to be a great fit. In this business, what comes around, goes around!'

Mix, mingle and meet

Because of our reliance on technology for communication, connecting with other writers, editors and PR professionals in person is more important than ever – especially for writers. Sure, social media sites, texting, emailing, video chatting and phone calls are helpful but nothing replaces the power of knowing someone in person. Luckily, there are many, many opportunities for travel writers to meet other like-minded travel professionals. Start with meet-ups in your city then graduate to bigger events.

Conferences are found all over the world. Eye for Travel (eyefortravel.com) is a fantastic website for learning about travel industry conferences, seminars and trade shows. As for blogger events Blog Conference Guide (blogconferenceguide.com) keeps up with blog and social media events.

Look at such gatherings as a chance to meet people IRL (in real life) whom you have only communicated with online, as well as a learning experience through attending informative sessions and socializing with other travel professionals.

MIX IT UP

Going to the same conference year after year is great for reconnecting with people, but in addition, make an effort to try a new event each year. Kimberly Button, author and freelance journalist (kimbutton.com) explains why:

> *'Industry events are wonderful networking opportunities, but they're not necessary every year. Many times the tourist organizations are the same every year, so pick an event at a location that's easy for your to get to, or at a location where you're excited to research and write many articles. Otherwise, don't waste your time, and the tourist organizations' time, by going to the same events year after year.'*

Have a plan

Social anxiety is a normal fear for some people. It can be intimidating to walk into a room knowing no one.

Luckily, today's social media world has allotted us the benefit for finding out who is going to be attending the same events so you at least have a common foundation with other attendees.

Here are some ways to go about having a fun and successful time at any travel writing event:

- Search for conference hashtags (eg: #TBEX) on Twitter for people talking about the upcoming event or join Facebook groups that have been created specifically for the gathering you are attending. Or better yet, start your own to get the conversation going.

- Make plans to meet up with people.

- After you meet a few people you will likely be introduced to their network of acquaintances.

- Look for other people who look uncomfortable. You won't be the only person who doesn't know anyone.

- Avoid being preoccupied with your Smartphone. It will be tempting to check your email or update your status, but when you're in a group setting make an effort to connect. If you're too involved with your electronics you're likely missing some great introductions.

- Dress appropriately. What to wear to events is always at the forefront of people's minds. Often the invitation will include the dress code. If that's not the case, assume business casual during the day and business in the evenings. Unless you're attending a travel conference that is offering casual day excursions, skip the jeans. If you're really at a loss, ask people who have attended the conference in previous years for some insight.

- Be confident. A strong handshake and a smile are all you need for any social setting. Remember these two things and the rest of your experience will fall into place.

- Be ready to network. Have your business cards within reach. Don't make your new contact wait as you dig through your coat or purse. Someone could easily scoop in and your chance to connect after the event could vanish. (See Chapter 13 for more on business cards.)

- Be tech savvy. While business cards are still being passed freely, business card swapping apps trends are on the rise. CardSwapp.com is one of many examples.

- Keep a pen and small notebook handy. You never know when you need to jot down notes for follow-ups or perhaps the person you're speaking with ran out of cards and wants to give you their email address or phone number.

- Use memory jogs. If you must, write down notes on the back of business cards to remind you later of important information.

Portraying confidence

Introducing yourself with good posture, a strong handshake and a smile will urge others to take you seriously regardless of your age or experience.

If this is your first event, there is no reason to share with people how inexperienced you are in writing or how little you've travelled, but rather share what experiences you do have. Nothing turns people off more than negative self talk. Of course, make an effort not to boast about your experiences. People don't care to talk to the obviously self-absorbed. Find a place somewhere in the middle. Besides, the best social advice I have is to be genuinely interested in the person you are speaking with at the moment. Possessing such a trait will make you naturally gleam with self-confidence.

DRESSING FOR THE OCCASION

Some events don't clarify what the dress code is. Similar to dressing for press trips, every event has its own vibe. Some conferences are casual while others are business or business casual. It's your job to find out what is acceptable during the day and evening events. Assume the evening events are a bit more formal than the sessions put on during the day. Aim to look polished and appropriate if the event is geared toward industry professionals. If the event is mainly geared toward writers, it's likely most people will be dressed down. Susan Farewell, President and Editor-in-Chief of Farewell Travels

(FarewellTravels.com), wrote an insightful post called Dos and Don'ts for Getting Invited on Press Trips for Travel Writers Exchange (travel-writers-exchange.com). Follow her advice on this topic: 'Don't perpetuate the starving writer syndrome. While you may think your laid-back style of dressing is reflective of your creative genius, it's not appropriate to show up at a 4- or 5-star hotel dressed as if you're a street musician.'

SOCIALIZE

Think of the last time you were at a party. Do you recall the natural networkers? They were the confident people flitting from person to person, shaking hands, connecting with each person in their own natural way and most likely exchanging business cards before moving on to their next greeting.

Perhaps you were the natural networker or maybe you were the wall flower, standing in the corner sipping your glass of merlot hoping to either be noticed or ignored. Either way, any type of gathering is an opportunity to meet others. Just because you're at a non-travel event doesn't mean you shouldn't network. In fact, getting out of the travel realm can open up doors you never thought possible. Perhaps you will meet someone who runs a restaurant in a destination you've been wanting to visit or maybe you will meet someone who is a relative of a local magazine's editor.

Doors open in the strangest places. Sometimes simply meeting people who have been to upcoming destinations can give you insight that you would have otherwise not known.

Better yet, industry travel-themed conferences and gatherings will make you realize and feel that you are part of something even bigger than you imagined.

Travel journalist Ramsey Qubein (RamseyQ.com) says:

> 'Travel writing really is about networking. Meeting other writers and professionals in the business is the best way to move forward in this business. You can pitch your heart out, but if you don't have a solid network of peers (editors, writers, public relations executives, etc.) it is a lot harder. Treat others with loyalty, integrity, and honesty, and they

will treat you in the same manner. The Golden Rule is alive and well in all industries ... including travel writing!'

Online networking

Despite all that's been said about face-to-face networking, don't discount online networking. Not only are there endless opportunities for travel writers, there is something out there for every niche. The 'find your tribe' advice has been swirling the writing waves for a few years now which is a modern way of saying birds of a feather flock together.

Don't be afraid of your competition, there really is strength in numbers and remember that the more defined your specialty the easier it is to support others.

Observing social media sites, online forums, even in-person conferences will show that while there are some overlaps of travel writing topics, the backpackers socialize most with other backpackers and the family travel writers say within their circles. One note about the internet: be judicious when posting anything online. The internet is forever and if you are caught disparaging someone there is a good chance your words will reach that person.

Thanks to the various online networking opportunities such as LinkedIn groups, Travel Media Pros and Travel Editors & Freelance Journalists, Travel Blog Exchange virtual networking is easy and convenient.

The joy of PR people

In my experience, public relations professionals are just that – professional. They are helpful, kind, generous with their time and make an effort to do what it takes to get their job done fairly and help you have the best outcome.

When you work with people in marketing or public relations be sure to treat them with kindness. They have a job to do as do you and they can help make your life much easier.

FILTERING PR

Even though my experience with publicists has been nothing but pleasant, sometimes we need to balance the time we spend on email. Media of all sorts eventually end up on dozens if not hundreds of PR email lists. At first it can be flattering to be included on a media list, but eventually, when you can't keep up with your inbox, it can be rather annoying and time-consuming – especially with emails from PR firms who send daily updates and follow-ups. Email can become a full-time job if we let it.

I receive many press releases and email blasts that are irrelevant to my work as a travel writer. Therefore, I've found it necessary to filter what makes it into my inbox. If you find yourself drowning in unsolicited information try these tactics to keep your inbox under control:

- ▶ Unsubscribe from useless newsletters or unwanted press releases. Look for an unsubscribe link at the bottom of the email. Alternatively, reply with a 'please unsubscribe me' message.

- ▶ When there is no way to unsubscribe, mark the email as spam. The emails in this file can still be scanned weekly to ensure you didn't miss any 'real' emails.

- ▶ With junk mail, if the first line of the email isn't addressed to me personally or if it looks like a generic salutation, bin it.

Focus points

Networking can be your ticket to travel writing success. Maintain and nurture the connections you make.

Always have a business card with you.

The internet is forever; use good judgement when posting anything online.

Respect publicists and remember they are there to help you.

Don't let your email inbox take more time than necessary.

Next step

The style and manner in which we network also says a lot about our personal brand. Upcoming Chapter 13 is going to help with the specifics as you develop your personal brand which in turn will help you develop a solid and respectable reputation.

The Importance of Self-Branding

In this chapter you will learn:

▶ *How to build a writer's platform*
▶ *How to write your bio*
▶ *How to brand yourself*
▶ *What to include on your business cards*
▶ *How to choose the right photo for your online image*

Today's travel writer relies on self-promotion as much as their writing skills. The online world has allowed strangers to take a peek at our online persona and it's very important that what you present to the world is exactly how you want to be known.

Have you Googled yourself lately? This sentence may appear to be a joke to many people, but for us writers it can reveal a number of things, including when our articles have been published and what people are saying about our work.

One of the joys of the internet is being able to track our online reputation and a helpful way of doing this is signing up for Google Alerts. This is how it works: anytime the phrase, name or word you request is published on the internet and Google discovers it you will receive an email with a link to the article or posting. Use this online tool to monitor anything else of interest such as niche travel topics or favourite authors.

You may also plug in your website or blog names or anything else that is associated with you. For example, if someone writes about you in their blog (perhaps they are referencing an article you wrote), it's nice to stop by the page and thank them for including or mentioning you in their piece.

Try it now

Monitor your online reputation by Googling your name under websites, images and videos. Does anything come up? If so, are you pleased?

Who are you?

Before you brand yourself you need to know what type of persona you want to portray and where you want your career to take you. Luckily, your online persona is something only you can develop. Identifying your goals, hopes and dreams will help in planning your path. Before the internet, unless you had your own magazine or newspaper column, the only branding that mattered was a writer's final product. Today, everyone has a personal brand and it is apparent through the various online outlets.

Build your bio

Your bio will evolve as you gain experience. It's fun to look back at former summaries and see how far you've come. Your bio should include the following:

▶ your byline name – if you go by a nickname rather than your legal name, list that

▶ your 'also known as' name (e.g. your social media handle)

▶ your job title – 'travel writer'

▶ your expertise – 'specializing in…'

▶ your biggest accomplishments – 'published in…,' awards, career titles, etc.

▶ your website

▶ contact information – email

Here is a fictitious example:

> *Jess Brown, aka the Caffeine Traveller, is a travel writer specializing in coffee and tea. She has been published in over 200 publications including* Coffee Today *magazine and* Tea Shops Around the World *and has been quoted for her expertise in the* New York Times, USA Today *and* Imbibe *magazine. You may learn more about her on [list website], email her at [list email address] and follow her on Twitter [handle].*

Every writer's bio is basic at first. With time you will be able to expand on your credentials, published titles and other interesting facts. When you're first starting you may not have any publications to list or media mentions. That's okay.

Editors may ask for one of several length bios: a short one- or two-line bio, 100 words or a longer 250+ words.

Branding

While we writers may not be trying to make the cover of *People* magazine as rock stars or paparazzi-sought actors we still need to be aware of what messages we are sending out to the world and mould our images into something that is appropriate for what we are attempting to accomplish. That is branding. This is very important today considering webcams seem to be on every corner, Twitter leaks new stories faster than news stations and 'friends' can post unflattering photos of us on Facebook at will.

Branding is more than a cartoon logo and a clever tag line. It's also about how you live and portray that to your readers. Dave Bouskill and Deb Corbeil of ThePlanetD.com explain:

> 'To be successful at travel blogging, you have to put in a lot of time networking and promoting yourself. To create a brand, you have to have a clear vision as to what you want to achieve. We focus on adventure travel, but our blog is about inspiring people to live their lives to the fullest. Adventure is for everyone and by facing our fears and sharing our experiences, we hope to encourage others to try something new.'

Remember this

No matter where you are – in person or online – how you present and conduct yourself is important.

Planning your platform

A writer's platform today is multidimensional compared to what it was twenty years ago. The more diverse your platform is, the more people you reach. Today, your fame, or access to it, is paramount in landing a book deal or even an agent.

Your platform should consist of your personal website, your professional blog (travel themed), publications you contribute to, conferences you speak at, radio and television opportunities. As was discussed in Chapter 10, websites and social media have contributed to the platform expansion. This includes Facebook, Twitter and any other relevant social media sites such as Google Plus, Pinterest, YouTube, Flickr and Tumbler to name a few.

The good news is anyone can build a personal platform on their own.

If you foresee a book in your future, you will especially want to be working on your platform. The former author platform consisted of speaking gigs, teaching classes and television appearances. But with the new wave of social media, publishers are expecting authors to have solid online platforms:

▶ **Twitter.** Some people have become as addicted to Twitter as they are to their morning java. You don't have to be on Twitter 24/7 to be involved. After all, professional writers need to make time to write. But do build an authentic following by joining in travel related conversations and commenting on other travellers' adventures.

▶ **Pinterest.** As a growing social media site, this photo-inspired platform can be used by writers to showcase their articles, photography, blog posts and, most of all, to contribute to self-branding. Glance at a writer's Pinterest page and you will see their personality shining through.

▶ **Facebook.** For a long time authors struggled with the dilemma whether to make their Facebook page business or personal. Luckily, the Fan Page has solved that problem. Instead of accepting offers to be 'friends' on Facebook, lead strangers to your Fan Page, but also be a fan of other travel writers and authors. You may also allow fans to subscribe to your feed without having to 'friend' them back.

Remember this

If your dream is to write a travel book, then a presence on all the social media platforms is vital long before you begin your book.

SAY CHEESE

Certainly you've seen the tacky and tasteless avatars on social media sites. If you want to be taken seriously, don't take that path. The only attention it will get you is, trust me, not the type you desire. Think tasteful.

You should have already Googled your name; now try it under 'images' and 'videos'. What comes up? Were you delighted with the search results? Next, take a peek at photos you've been tagged in on Facebook or other sites. Did you have to make some calls to friends to have them remove some unflattering photos of you?

As a travel writer, you don't have to don a suit or string of pearls for your 'this is me' photos. However, if you want to take the professional route and start speaking at conferences, it's nice to polish your image and have professional photos taken. After all, a backpacker dressed like a business man makes for brand confusion. When I was featured as a travel expert in *USA Today,* the journalist writing the piece requested a high-resolution photo of my daughter and me. Luckily, I own a Nikon which produces high-res photos and we were able to take one and send it over.

Choose with care the photos that accompany your online bios. The social media platforms that you use purely for personal reasons are not included in the 'don't use' list, but remember to keep the photos tasteful since your image is still reflected in your online persona.

When you attend conferences or other face-to-face meetings your followers should be able to recognize you from your online avatar. Believe it or not, this is self-branding. Here are some general rules for posting photos on your professional social media sites (the key word is professional. Your personal Facebook page can break most or all of these tips, but be judicious):

► Don't use old photos of yourself. Make sure the image you use is current and looks like you. Even if you've gained 20 pounds in the last year or coloured your hair, use an updated photo. It helps people recognize you in person, proves your authenticity, and shows that you are confident enough to be yourself and not wishing you looked like you did in college. Not long ago I was recognized in the airport from my LinkedIn profile. The reason: I make an effort to use updated photos that look like me as I currently am and you should, too.

► Don't use poor quality photos. Blurry or amateur photos are distracting.

► Don't use photos of your pet, children or you and your spouse (unless you work as a team).

► Don't use photos of you in a wild, weekend environment.

Your personal website

The most valuable platform on the web isn't what publication you were published in. It's your personal website. Your website should be 100 per cent about you. Not your kids, husband, parents or pets. If you specialize in pet or family travel that's fine, but there is no reason to feature your kids or pets directly. This space should concentrate on your accomplishments, background and most of all how you can assist the person reading. Your goal should be to tempt the readers to want to learn more about you, hire you or connect with you.

The most important details to include when building your website are:

► Name

► Photo

► Contact information

▶ Your published credits, awards and background or career information if it's relevant

Make your website yours: personalize it.

What's your tag line?

Branding experts have varying opinions on whether individuals should give themselves a tag line. Some experts say let the media brand you, while others say you should sum up your expertise in a few words and let the world know.

As a newbie, give yourself time to discover your specialties, strengths and goals and let your creative line evolve. If you already have something perfect in mind, then by all means go for it. I change mine every now and then. Right now I use Travelling with Flair. But, that could change next week. Have fun with it!

Your image

Imagine you are being interviewed by your favourite talk show host. What's the vibe of your show? Is it a conservative morning show or is it a wild and trendy setting? What are you wearing? What are you talking about? Are you a go-to expert or a trend-setter?

How you appear online is the same thing. (Don't worry if you have no interest in being on television, this is simply an exercise.)

Think of all of all of the travel show hosts. Each person has their own style, dress and language that work for then. Even though you will be communicating from the page your writing and image will be revealed through both words and photos.

Sarcastic comments, careless cursing and political ranting work for some people, while others simply can't pull it off. Instead they come off crass and unrefined. You need to find what works for you. Are you creative in your process, such as posting photos of your travels, or are you more inspirational sending positive messages via your social media platform? There is no right or wrong way to do it; there's only your authenticity and people can see that.

If you're only promoting yourself without any regard for your audience, your followers will lose interest (unless you are a celebrity). If you observe some of the top social media names, they engage their audience by communicating and offering worthy information that helps and educates those interested in their topic.

While there's certainly room for everyone in travel writing, it's not easy to stand out. That's why paying attention to the image you present to the world is imperative. Let your style and life evolve and let your personality glow.

Every writer, regardless of their genre, has a style. That style is influenced by education, experience and dedication. As we grow and age what we used to produce naturally changes. Our topics of interest will also lean in different directions. That's how we know we're on the right path, we're writing in the moment about our latest passions.

When I first started writing, my stories revolved around events and stories that occurred during my early years as a flight attendant. If you follow my published stories you will note that as time went on, my interests and experiences changed. My creative non-fiction stories faded and my writing turned into practical travel tips about flying pregnant, which transitioned into flying with children. As my life changed so did my interests which in turn made an impact on what I was writing.

I urge you to tap into what fascinates you then write about it. If you have a zeal for a certain subject it will show in your writing which will nicely accompnay your image.

Keep a media page

As I mentioned in Chapter 2, the number of publications I have contributed to has helped enhance my expertise, but, more than this, every article I have produced has helped to mould my personal brand. If you've appeared on TV, in articles or spoken on panels at conferences, let the world know on your media page, then link to the proof.

Try it now

Launch your own resumé website – preferably with your name or a close variation.

On your website include:

✳ an 'About me' page with your photo
✳ a 'Contact' page (with your email address)
✳ a 'Publications' page showing your list of published credits; you can organize your credits by topic if they're not all travel topics (business, parenting, health, etc.)

Update the page every time you get published or have something new to add. You may also include a page with your photos, media mentions, list of travels or other interests that are relevant.

Recommendations

Don't discredit the benefits of LinkedIn, Facebook's BranchOut and other professional social media sites. These websites allow for contacts to sing the praises of professional peers. If you already have some references from others, pull the flattering quotes then ask the author if you may use them on your personal sites, too.

If you don't have any recommendations, there are a couple of ways of getting them. First, ask for them. There should be no shame in asking others for recommendation if they are warranted. Another way is write recommendations for others. If you think back over your work experiences there will be plenty of people who you can compliment and there is a good chance they will happily return the favour.

Your name

As a new writer, there is nothing more thrilling than seeing your byline in a publication for the first time.

As a professional writer your 'real' name is what will be remembered. Some writers opt to use their birth name, while others opt for their nicknames. The choice is yours. It is, after all, what goes in the byline of every article you write.

Social media has allowed us to get creative and have fun with our handles and avatars. When an editor needs to fill an assignment, they will be calling you by your name and not your handle. Thus, make sure that if you're going to do something catchy with your brand and/or website that it works with your name, like Dave and Deb did with Planet D or John DiScala and his memorable moniker which is also his website's name: Johnny Jet.

Remember this

Many new writers wonder if a pen name is necessary when starting their writing career. Very few people I know use a pen name unless they write for various genres. If you're known in your field as a respectable professional but also write racy romance novels, it would certainly be advisable to use a pen name for your novels. However, if you specialize in various non-fiction topics there is no reason for you use different names for different topics.

Try it now

Open a Google Account – try it with your own name, a shortened version or a creative spin on your name – then sign up for Google Alerts. If you have a common name, write combinations, such as 'By Beth Blair' or 'Writer Beth Blair' or 'Beth Blair Travel' that distinguish you from other people in other professions who share your name.

Portfolio

By now you should realize the benefits of having an accessible online portfolio, but it's also a good idea to have a physical portfolio you can hold and show off to anyone who requests it. If you have a number of print clips it may be tempting to cut these out, use a hole puncher and throw them in a binder. I've seen writer portfolios done like this and it's best to avoid this tactic. It looks tacky. Newspaper turns yellow after a while and magazine pages can easily tear, especially if the book gets a wide readership. Instead, scan your article (as well as the cover of the magazine and the index with your article listed) and print using a high-quality printer with vibrant ink at your local office supply store. Then, slide your clips into a clean, plastic protective sleeve with binder holes, and then place the pages in your binder. You will appear professional and polished when the new editor you're meeting for lunch asks to see your work. And, yes, that does happen.

Business cards

There's nothing more embarrassing than to be asked for a business card and not have one. Even when you're first starting out, presenting a professional card complete with your name, title and contact information guarantees a professional and confident image.

Having something physical to exchange with new acquaintances can help immensely when attending an event. Not only will the business cards help jog your memory after you get home but your name will also stay with others long after the affair.

Make it a point to read the card the moment someone hands you theirs. Not only does it show that you are genuinely interested in them but reading the card can help you remember their name and learn something about them such as where they live, what business they're in and what image they are presenting to the world.

Business cards are wonderful conversation starters. Logo, quality and images or quotes on the back of the card have all led to interesting discussions.

Try it now

Order your business cards. When trying to decide the ideal size business card there are a few things to consider. Do you want to stand out with miniature business cards, traditional-sized cards or oversized postcards?

Where you live or are travelling should determine the standard card size to ensure the card fits in card holders. If you live in the United States, the usual business card size is 3.5 × 2 in

(89 × 51 mm), whereas in the UK and Europe the average business card is 85 × 55 mm (3.37 × 2.12 in). In Japan business cards are normally 91 × 55 mm.

► Ordering cards in bulk will guarantee you always have enough cards and it will save you money.

► Include your real name, contact information (email, phone, address), websites and top social media site handles.

► Keep cards with you all of the time. You never know who you may meet in unexpected places.

► Leave the reverse side free so you always have room to take notes or give more information if requested.

► If you have a professional logo designed with your name or photo then put it to use.

Focus points

The persona you put out on the internet is how you are perceived professionally.

Travel writing may be casual, but you should still present yourself professionally.

Never be caught without a business card.

Use appropriate photos online.

As a writer, think about ways you can develop your platform.

Next step

Staying up to date on the latest travel and tourism news and trends can be time-consuming but by getting involved in organizations and attending conferences you will always be in the know. Chapter 14 will offer suggestions and also cover a few other tit-bits that travel writers should keep in mind as they pursue their dream career.

Staying in the Know and Other Extras

In this chapter you will learn:

- ▶ *The benefits of attending conferences*
- ▶ *Why you should join travel writing organizations*
- ▶ *How to handle envious friends*
- ▶ *Safety issues to be aware of as a travel writer*
- ▶ *How being a travel writer can lead to other career opportunities*

With all of the media transitions occurring it's important for professional travel writers to keep up with industry changes, hot events and networking opportunities. This final chapter will show the budding travel writer how to keep up with travel writing trends

Conferences

As discussed in Chapter 12, conferences are one of the most attractive network outlets but such gatherings are also appealing since the panels and presentations usually cover the most groundbreaking topics, latest trends, new products and interesting information.

It is impossible to attend every conference. Not only is attending conferences costly, sometimes the same speakers appear regurgitating the same information.

To know whether a conference is right for you:

▶ Find out what type of people will be at the conference. Are attendees other writers, editors, PR representatives, industry insiders or the public?

▶ Weigh the benefits of attending the event: networking, knowledge of new trends, etc.

TRAVEL-THEMED CONFERENCES AND SHOWS

▶ Adventure Travel World Summit: adventuretravel.biz

▶ Book Passage Travel Writers & Photographers Conference: bookpassage.com

▶ Boston Globe Travel Show: bostonglobetravelshow.com

▶ IMEX Frankfurt: imex-frankfurt.com

▶ IMEX America: imexamerica.com

▶ Los Angeles Times Travel Show: events.latimes.com/travelshow

▶ New York Times Travel Show: nyttravelshow.com

▶ PhoCusWright: phocuswright.com

- Social Media Strategies for Travel: eyefortravel.com
- Travel and Adventure: adventureexpo.com
- Travel Blog Exchange (TBEX): travelblogexchange.com
- Travel Bloggers Unite: travelbloggersunite.com
- Travel Massive: travelmassive.com/events

Case study: Benefits of conferences for travel writers

Jody Halsted entered the world of travel blogging after her first child was born. In the past six years she has worked with companies such as Walt Disney World, Omni Hotels, MegaBus and numerous CVBs, sharing travel tales on her own websites: FamilyRambling.com and IrelandwithKids.com. She also writes weekly for Uptake Attractions, bi-monthly travel articles for *Blissfully Domestic* magazine and has written for *We Just Got Back*, *Ciao Bambino* and the *Des Moines Register*. Jody is active in new media, talking travel on Twitter (@iatraveler) and host of the Iowa-based Social Technology Conference (formerly I_Blog).

'When you are beginning any new profession it is always advisable to surround yourself with people who are where you want to be in two to five years. Attending a conference is the best way to do that. This puts you within their sphere of influence, where you can meet someone you admire, learn things you don't know and rub elbows with people you might have difficulty connecting with otherwise.

In the realm of travel writing conferences, you'll have the opportunity to meet other writers, which is a great way to get insider tips and tricks, but you want to move to the figurative "head of the table" and meet the sponsors, editors and companies who are there. Introduce yourself and ask questions. Find a common ground outside their product and create a relationship that isn't based on how they can help you. Some of my longest term travel partnerships have been based on shared interests.

But don't limit yourself to travel conferences. If you plan to work online a blog or internet conference can connect you to people who can help you network online, build a spectacular website or walk you through the world of social media. Even companies that may not be in your niche

Organizations

As a member of Society of American Travel Writers (SATW) I can vouch for the advantages of being part of a professional organization. It's fun, informative, and great for networking. I'm not the only who feels this way. Maralyn D. Hill (theepicureanexplorer.com) suggests new writers explore local writing groups and associations:

> *'It will take clips to be accepted into the better-known organizations including International Food Wine & Travel Writers Association (IFWTWA), Society of American Travel Writers (SATW) and American Society of Journalists and Authors (ASJA). There are more organizations; these are just the ones I highly recommend. Naturally, I'm partial to IFWTWA, as I'm President. We have advanced to stay current with technology, run a conference and two to four media trips a year, have an online profile where you can showcase your clips, Global Writes – our magazine where you can submit articles, as well as our monthly newsletter, Press Pass.'*

Hill also points out that IFWTWA offers an Excellence Award Scholarship for emerging writers.

> *'I personally find Press Pass and our online profile two of the most valuable benefits, with our conference being third. Every month, Press Pass offers several pages on different paying markets, press trips that are available and a myriad of information. We have members who get all of their assignments through Press Pass leads and develop relationships with various editors. Others go back and work past issues, which are all available online in our members only section of our website. Writing organizations will provide you with insight to the market and contacts. A journalist needs both.'*

The future of your career

The exciting thing about travel writing is it can take you around the world physically and up the career ladder figuratively.

Some writers start off penning articles in their basement and before they know it, they're sitting in a magazine office with a name plate on their door that says 'editor'. Chris Anderson of the Huffington Post is an example of someone who worked his way up the ladder:

> 'I got started in the travel writing and editing field when I moved to Shanghai, China in 2006. I had no previous experience in the field and started from complete scratch. I did a bit of freelance writing my first year in Shanghai, then got hired as editor of a new, small English language lifestyle magazine that just launched. Getting that first editorial job was really my "big break". The managing editor took a chance on me, and I ended up learning more in my year at the publication than I would have over three years in an 'entry level' role in the US. It was that position and Asia experience that put me on track to get hired as the Associate Editor of CNNGo.com, and later as Senior Travel Editor for Huffington Post Travel and AOL Travel, and most recently as Senior Editor, Huffington Post.'

Safety first

One downfall to travelling frequently, if you live alone, is that you need to take precautions when it comes to your home and ensuring its safety but you should also take precautions when you're on the road. When you're travelling and using social media to promote your travels, you're announcing to the world that you're not at home. Keep this in mind and make plans accordingly by installing a security alarm, hiring a house sitter, alerting the local authorities that you will be gone or asking the neighbours to watch your home while you're away.

TRAVEL WRITERS BEWARE
Because travel writers are frequently away from home it can make them and their friends and family easy targets for email scams.

Hijacked accounts can result in loss of control of email, social media accounts and even bank accounts if emails containing private information are opened.

To avoid being victim of an online travel writer scam:

▸ Keep as much personal information as you can private (phone numbers, home address).

▸ Make your online passwords complex by combining letters, numbers and special characters. Avoid obvious passwords like birthdays, anniversaries and nicknames.

Health

Travelling too much can trigger exhaustion and frustration. When you arrive at your destination you may not have much time to adjust to your new time zone. Drink plenty of fluids, get plenty of rest and take care of your overall health before and during your travels. You don't want to get stranded somewhere with an illness. While the actual trips may be great fun, looming deadlines can be stressful and recovery from a trip can take days or even weeks.

The 'green-eyed monster'

A book about being a writer isn't complete without the topic of writer envy. This little monster creeps out from time to time, especially when writer friends' careers soar or someone on the same level suddenly leaps to a higher status and you feel left behind. Awards, prestigious trip invitations or high-paying assignments are just a few times the feelings of inadequacy or jealousy may kick in.

I've watched writers wallow in self-pity or act out in a fit of rage as they hear about other writers' success and opportunities while moaning, 'why not me?' Don't be that person:

▸ Remember, you are only as good as the company you keep. If the people around you are on their way to success you are not far behind.

- ▶ Genuinely feel the joy for other writers. Support and congratulate their accomplishments. Hopefully, they will do the same for you when the time comes

- ▶ Ask other writers out for coffee to exchange writer stories. You may learn something.

On the other hand, you may be the person who leaps to success only to find your peers are glaring at your success from behind their laptops. Don't take it personally if you become the target of jealous eyes. Your success is your own. Claim it and rejoice. You've earned it.

As you begin your journey...

Remember it is okay to make mistakes. Simply learn from them and move on. With every word you write and article you sell your writing will improve and your confidence will thrive. But most importantly, remember as you break into travel writing, never give up. Belief is your stongest force.

Taking it Further

WRITER ORGANIZATIONS

American Society of Journalists and Authors (ASJA): asja.org

Australian Society of Travel Writers (ASTW): astw.org.au

British Guild of Travel Writers (BGTW): bgtw.org

Canadian Association of Journalists (CAJ): caj.ca

Chartered Institute of Journalists (CIoJ): cioj.co.uk

International Society for Travel Writing (ISTW): istw-travel.org

National Union of Journalists (NUJ): nuj.org.uk

National Writers Union (NWU): nwu.org/

Society of American Travel Writers (SATW): satw.org

Society of Authors (SOA): societyofauthors.org/

Travel Journalists Guild (TJG): tjgonline.com

WRITER WEBSITES

Find journalist jobs: JournalismJobs.com

Journalism news in the UK: Journalism.co.uk

Freelance writing website: FreelanceWriting.com

Freelance writing community (FLX): FreelanceSuccess.com

Mediabistro is dedicated to all writing/creative/content professionals: Mediabistro.com

Service and community for travel writing professionals: MediaKitty.com

Travel media news distribution site: TravMedia.com

Dedicated to new media travel writing: Travelwriting2.com

Community for travel writers, bloggers and journalists: Travel-writers-exchange.com/

Freelance writing ezine: WritersWeekly.com

Extensive website for writers: WritersDigest.com

Source for where and how to sell your writing:
WritersMarket.com

BOOKS

▶ References

Alderson, Alf, *Ultimate Surfing Destinations* (John Wiley, 2010)

Alderson, Alf, Wilson, Cameron, and Williams, Christian, *Rough Guide to the Rocky Mountains* (Rough Guides, 2002)

Biernacki, Henry, *No More Heroes* (AuthorHouse, 2010)

Bryson, Bill, *Neither Here Nor There* (William Morrow Paperbacks, 1993)

Bryson, Bill, *The Lost Continent: Travels in Small Town America* (Harper Perennial, 1990)

Castleman, Amanda, *Greece, A Love Story* (Seal Press, 2007)

Castleman, Amanda, *Rome in Detail* (Rizzoli, 2003)

Clowers, Anya, *Jet with Kids* (Jet Seven, 2006)

Deckers, Erik, and Falls, Jason, *No Bullshit Social Media* (Que Publishing, 2011)

Deckers, Erik, and Lacy, Kyle, *Branding Yourself* (2nd edn, Que Publishing, 2012)

Gilbert, Elizabeth, *Eat, Pray, Love* (Viking, 2006)

Gray Faust, Chris, *Philadelphia Essential Guide for iPhone and iPad* (Sutro Media, 2011)

Hart, Melissa, *Gringa: A Contradictory Girlhood* (Seal Press, 2009)

Jarolim, Edie, *Frommer's San Antonio & Austin* (6th edn, 2005)

Jarolim, Edie, *The Complete Idiot's Travel Guide To Mexico's Beach Resorts* (Alpha Books, 1999)

Jarolim, Edie, *Arizona For Dummies* (4th edn, John Wiley, 2007)

Krakauer, Jon, *Into the Wild* (Anchor, 1997)

McCartney, Scott, *The Wall Street Journal Guide to Power Travel: How to Arrive with Your Dignity, Sanity, and Wallet Intact* (HarperBusiness, 2009)

Potts, Rolf, *Vagabonding: An Uncommon Guide to the Art of Long-Term World Travel* (Villard Books, 2002)

Schneider, G. Michael, *On the Other's Guy's Dime* (Tasora Books, 2010)

Wortley Montagu, Lady Mary, *The Turkish Embassy Letters* (new edn, Virago, 1994)

▶ **Travel writing**

Brewer, Robert Lee, *Writer's Market 2013* (Writer's Digest, 2012)

George, Don, *The Lonely Planet Guide to Travel Writing* (Lonely Planet, 2nd Edition, 2009)

Leffel, Tim, *Travel Writing 2.0: Earning Money from your Travels in the New Media Landscape* (Splinter Press, 2010)

Spalding, Lavinia, *Writing Away: A Creative Guide to Awakening the Journal-Writing Traveler* (Travelers' Tales, 2009)

ONLINE WRITING CLASSES

Online writing classes are good because it doesn't matter where in the world you are. As long as you have an internet connection you can take a writing class!

Matador U: matadoru.com/

The Travel Writer's Life: thetravelwriterslife.com/

Writers Online Classes: writersonlineclasses.com/

The Writer's Workshop: thewritersworkshop.net/travel

Amanda Castleman: amandacastleman.com/classes.html

Index

accommodation 31
accountability 8
activity level 8
adaptability 8
adventure travel 29–30
adventurous nature 8
airlines 30
  airline miles 87
Alderson, Alf 31
allure of travel writing 6–7
Anderson, Chris 76–77, 110–11, 138, 190
anecdotes 150
angles 110–11
anthologies 119–20
approaching editors 3, 105–15
apps 71–72
Arndt, Gary 177
articles
  anecdotes 150
  beginnings 145–47
  main part 147–48
  ending 149–51
  humour 150
  outlines 144
  purpose of 132
  reselling 122
  rights 122–23
  summarizing 150
  timing of submission 116–17
  titles 145
  transitions 148
  types of 107–09
authoritative writing 33
availability to questions 36
aviation 30

backing up 17, 183
back packing experience 26

Badertscher, Vera Marie 32
Ball, Don 12–13
'best of' articles 30
Biernacki, Henry 52
biography building 203
blogs 60, 62, 68, 82–83, 120, 153–71
  appearance 157, 166
  audience appeal 156
  blogger personality 166
  branding 165–67
  content 167
  domain names 165
  and earnings 162
  essential ingredients of 169–70
  guest blogging 171
  logos 166
  marketing/promotion of 156
  media kit 160–62
  multi-bloggers 168
  and networking 159–60
  overuse of 167
  promoting 164–65
  purpose 170
  quantity 156
  and readers 167
  review writing 163
  successful 156–58
  and travel experience 157
  typos 157
  valuable content 156
  vlogging 183–85
  and websites 154–55
  work entailed in 158
BOB (back of book) articles 107
book contracts 48
book rights 122
books
  fiction vs non-fiction 51–52
  publication in 46–49

types of 47–48
on writing 14
boomer generation travel 27
Bouskill, Dave 155, 157, 170, 204
Branch Out 210
break-in tips 9–10
business cards 212–13
business sense 9
business travel 29

careers in travel writing 219
case studies
  the angle 111
  approaching editors 113–14
  apps 71–72
  blog branding 165–67
  blogging 169–70
  blogging and networking 159–60
  break-in tips 9–10, 169–170
  co-working 12–13
  conferences for travel writers
    217–18
  ebook publishing 69–71
  editor's point of view 62–63
  expertise 24
  fiction travel writing 52–53
  getting published 50–51
  guidebook writing 48–49
  multimedia assignment adventures
    186–87
  personal niches 34
  personal passions 32
  photography in social media 177
  pitching tricks 109–10
  press trips 84–86, 93–95
  qualities of travel writer 135–37
  social media 179–80
  travel opportunities 16–17
  travel writing tips 53–54
  writing and self-editing 139–41
Castleman, Amanda 139–41
challenge 25–26
childhood experience 25

clichés 138
Clowers, Anya 23
co-working 12–13
competitive pricing 70
computer backup 17, 183
conferences 193–97, 216–18
contact maintenance 192–93
contact sharing 193
content farms 65–66
Corbeil, Deb 155, 157, 170, 204
courtesy 9
coverage 82
creativity 36, 102
cruises 34
culinary trail travel 29
curiosity 8
CVB (Convention and Visitor Bureaus)
  92–93

deadline keeping 127–28, 136
Deckers, Eric 158
descriptive words 145–47
digital magazines 73
distractions, social media 178
domain names 165
Dragon Naturally Speaking
  software 9
dressing for occasions 196
drinks trail travel 29

earnings for travel writing 4–5, 7
ebooks 5–6, 67–71
editing 62–63, 128–29
  self-editing 137–41
editorial calendars 116
editors
  advantages of having 128–29
  approach to 3, 105–15
  connecting with 118–20
  hooks for 112
  introduction to 3
  negotiating with 121–22
  requirements of 103

responses from 67, 117, 120, 124–25
Eisenberg, Paul 24, 93
electronic applications (apps) 71–72
electronic books (ebooks) 5–6, 67–71
email 11, 15, 198–99
England, Angela 68–69
Espsëter, Anna Maria 103
essays 109
excitement of travel 7
exclamation marks 138–39
expatriates 26
expertise 22–24, 26–32, 33
eye-catching beginnings 145–47

Facebook 175, 205
fact-checking 76–77
factual accuracy 115
FAM (familiarization) trips see press trips
family press trips 80
family travel 27–28
Faust, Chris Gray 84–86
features articles 107–08
fiction travel writing 52–53
finder's fees 127
Finley-Bajak, Carrie 155, 175
flexibility of travel-writing career 7
FOB (front of book) articles 107
forums, online social media 179, 191
free travel 4
freebies 92
fun of travel writing 7

gay travel 29
George, Don 113
getting published 50–51
girlfriend getaways 31
Glatt, Jen 42
Google Alerts 202, 211
grammar 136
Groene, Janet 83
group press trips 78
guest blogging 171

guests on press trips 81
guidebooks 47–49
guidelines for writers 104–05, 111, 128

Halstead, Jodi 217
Harrington, Candy 25–26
Hart, Melissa 32
hashtags 174
health issues 220
Heller, Carolyn B. 190
helpfulness 36
Hill, Maralyn D. 9–10
home office 11–12
homeschooling 30
honeymoon travel 31–32
hooks to editor 112
how-to books 48
Huang, Nellie 67, 73
Hull, Donna 27, 64
human interest articles 108
humour 150

iBookstore 69
image 208–09
Imboden, Durant 60, 65
individual press trips 78–79
interview sound bites 36
interviewing sources 95–96
introduction to editors 3
invoices 123–24

Jarolim, Edie 135–37
Jenkins, Keith 165

KDP Select 71
keywords 70
kill fees 123
'kill your darlings' 139
Kindle 67, 69, 70

Lane, Sharon Hurst 61
latest travel trends 77
Leffel, Tim 23, 62

letter of introduction (LOI) 126
LinkedIn 176–77, 210
literary agents 53
local locations 43–44
local publications 42–43
loops 149

magazines 41–44, 54, 73
Mandel, Pam 55–56
manners on press trips 81–82
market identification 100, 102
media discounts 87
media pages 35, 209
media trips *see* press trips
meeting deadlines 8
Miner, Jennifer 162
mistakes 221
    correction 67
multigenerational travel 28
multimedia assignment adventures
        186–87
myths of travel writing 3–6

narrative travel books 47
national magazines 43
negotiation with editors 121–23
Nelson, Amy 102, 109
networking 14, 113
    and blogging 159–60
    helping others 190
    importance of 190–99
    online 198
new expectations 66
newspapers 41–44
niches 25, 34, 83, 94, 137
non-profit organizations 55
non-travel assignments 55
Nook 69

objective writing 135
observation 136
office equipment 14, 16
one-time rights 122

online library 15–16
online mistake correction 67
online networking 198
online portfolio 211
online printing 63–65
online rights 122
online scams 219–20
online travel guides 65
opportunities 103–04
organization 8
organizations 191, 218, 222
Orwoll, Mark 41, 144
other incomes 5
outdoors activity travel 30
outlines 144

packing checklist 17–19
passports 83, 95
payment for travel writing 4–5, 7
perks 7, 92
personal interests 40
personality of travel writers 7–8
persuasive writing 134–35
Pfeuffer, Charyn 109
photography 36, 102
    backing up 183
    professional tips 185
    in social media 177, 182–88
Pinterest 205
plagiarism 129
platform planning 205–07
PO box 15
popular print 41–44
portfolios 211
positive replies 120–21
Potts, Rolf 33, 55, 63–64
PR people 198–99
practical travel 28
pre-trip pitch 103
press trips 4, 55, 77–97
    airline miles 87
    benefits of 80
    case studies 84–86, 93–95

dressing for 89, 90
freebies/perks 92
interviewing sources 95–96
manners during 81
media discounts 87
myths 87–88
negative aspects 81
PR 93–95
scepticism during 91
types of 77–80
unexpected costs 89–92
pricing 70
printers 14
professional organizations 218
professionalism 22–24, 68, 112
profiles articles 108
promoting ebooks 70
promotional gifts 7
proofreading 141
publications, knowledge of 107–10
publicists 93
publicity 68
publishers
contact with *see* editors
websites 5, 104–05, 109

Qubein, Ramsey 28–29, 197
query letters 105–15.
quotations 149

reading other writers 44–46
references/recommendations 126, 137
reflective writing 132–34
regional magazines 43
regional rights 122
rejections 67, 124–25.
reputation 126
research 76–77, 103
on press trips 82
reselling articles 122
review writing 163
road office 15
round-up articles 108–09

round-ups 30
Rowe, Diana 65–66

safety 219–20
Sambuchino, Chuck 53
samples of work 119
satisfaction of travel writing 7
scanners 14
Scarborough, Sheila 179
searching hashtags 174
self-branding 202–13
self-editing 137–41
self-motivation 8
self-publishing 49–50, 60–61
ebooks 68
selling yourself 113
senses in writing 132–34
SEO (search engine optimization) 66, 164
service articles 108
Shisler, Tim 22, 190
sidebar articles 108
Smith, Dana Lynn 69–70
Sniadak, Dave 185
social anxiety 194–97
social media 174–80, 205–09
socializing 197
solo travel 26–27, 79
sound bites 36
spas 28
specialist how-to books 48
specialization 35, 60
specialized press trips 79
speculative submissions 126
spelling 136
spirit trail travel 29
sport travel 30
subsidized trips 4
swag (promotional gifts) 7

target audience 100–101
theme parks 28
thesaurus 138

timing submissions 116–17
topic selection 68
topics, limiting number of 112
tourism boards 92–93
trade magazines 44
traditional press trips 78
Tran, Minh 71–72
transitions 148
travel apps 71–72
travel expenses 54
travel literature articles 109
travel perks 7, 92
travel safety 219–20
travel trends 77
travel-themed conferences and shows 216–18
travel-writing organizations 191, 218, 222
Twitter 174–75, 178, 192, 205
Twitter trips 79

visual images 36
vlogging 183–85

weblogs see blogs
websites 60–61, 104–05, 109, 222
and blogs 154–55, see also blogs
wedding travel 31–32
Williams, Kara 190
Wilson, Benét J. 25
word repetition 138
writer envy 220–21
writers' guidelines 104–05, 111, 128
Writer's Market 100
writing style 46
writing tools 9

young adult travel 27